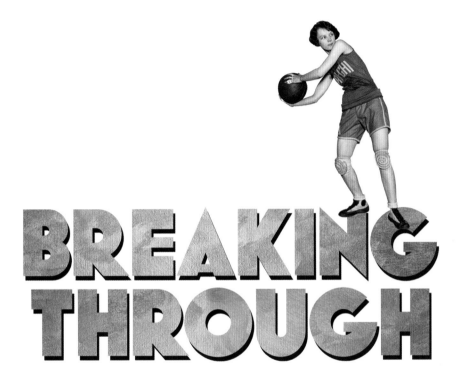

BREAKING THROUGH

BREAKING

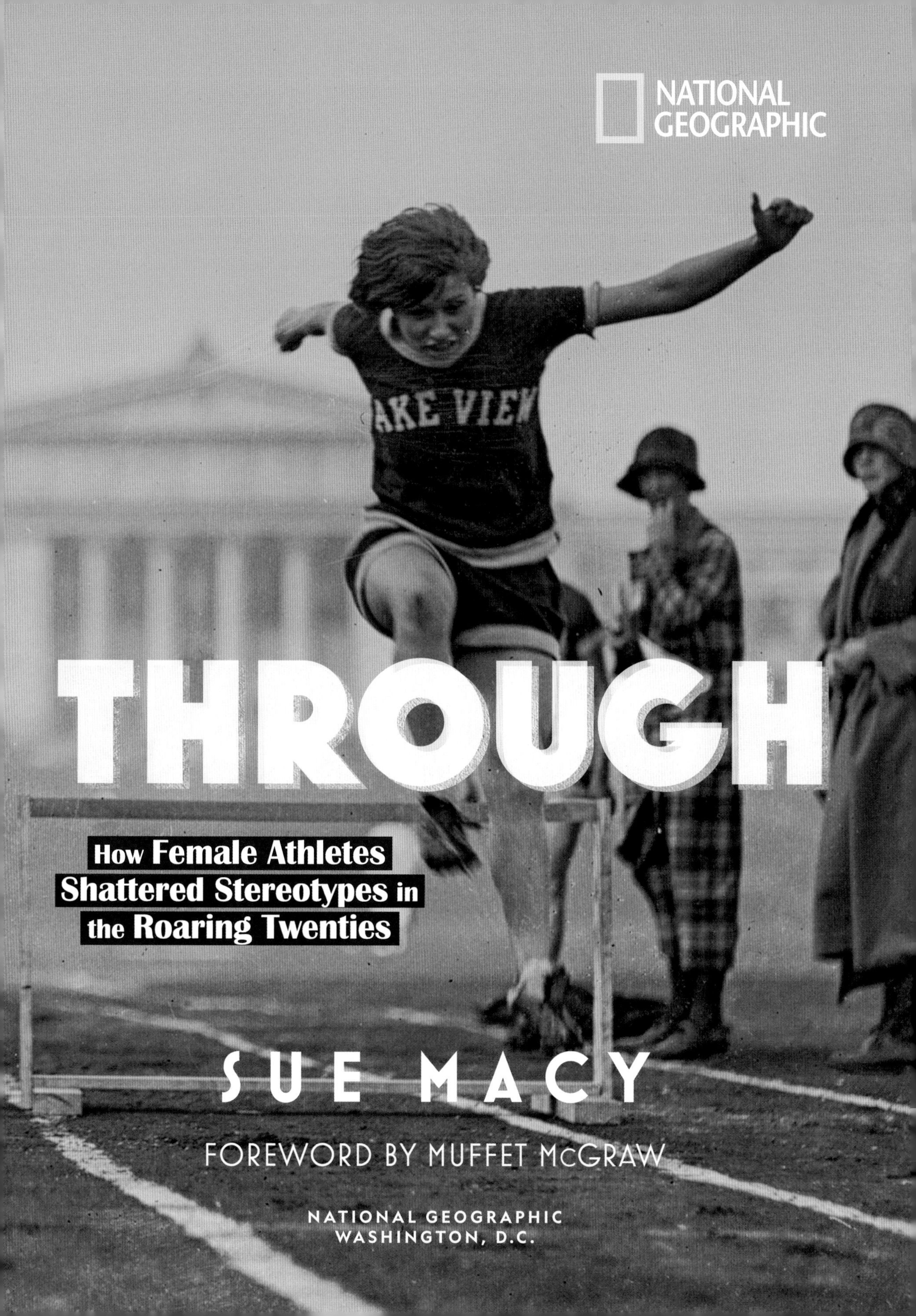

NATIONAL GEOGRAPHIC

THROUGH

How Female Athletes Shattered Stereotypes in the Roaring Twenties

SUE MACY

FOREWORD BY MUFFET McGRAW

NATIONAL GEOGRAPHIC
WASHINGTON, D.C.

CONTENTS

Dust jacket/front cover: **Sprinter Wanda Danley of Oakland, California, crosses the finish line in October 1925. Just a few weeks before, Danley had electrified the track world by beating champion Helen Filkey in the 100-yard dash.**

Half-title page**: Kathy Miller of the championship Tri-Chi Chicago girls basketball team, 1925**

Title page**: Track standout Norma Zilk (right) of Chicago's Lake View High School leads Margaret and Elizabeth Sheffield in a 1924 hurdles race.**

Right**: Spanish tennis star Lilí Álvarez hits a shot at Wimbledon in 1926. Álvarez won championships in ice-skating as well as tennis and wrote a book in English titled *Modern Lawn Tennis*.**

FOREWORD

— MUFFET McGRAW —

Head Coach, Notre Dame University
Women's Basketball

O**pportunities for women in sports** have come a long way since the 1920s. Back then women couldn't even go to the University of Notre Dame, let alone participate in sports there. It may be hard to imagine today, when almost all colleges are coed and female students have a host of sports to choose from, but for much of the 20th century, being a girl who loved sports could be a pretty frustrating and lonely experience.

But that didn't stop me from playing. Growing up, I was always the only girl playing basketball down at the playground with the guys. Thanks to Title IX*, I was lucky enough to go to college and play the sport that I loved. We certainly weren't treated like college basketball players are today, nor were we given the same amenities the men's team had. They were bussed to games, we drove our own cars. They were given practice uniforms that a manager washed for them every day, sneakers, and plenty of media attention. We wore our own clothes that we washed ourselves, bought our own sneakers, and the media barely knew we had a team. Practice times were constantly changing as we had to wait for the men's varsity and junior varsity teams to finish practice before we could take the court. But that was 1970, and fortunately, things have improved since then.

Sports is such an important part of life, for girls and boys. It teaches us how to work with others and how to come back from failures. As a coach, I can learn a lot about a player when I see how she reacts to losing. A few years ago, our team was undefeated in our conference until we lost a game by almost 40 points—on national TV. We were humiliated. The score was 100-67, the worst loss in our program's history, which goes all the way back to 1977. And I truly believe that loss is why we ended up winning the national championship the same year. We took stock and rebounded from it. We came from behind in our very next game and went on to win.

*For more on this law, see page 82.

Athletes need to learn how to battle through tough situations. Many of the athletes in this book had to fight simply to play the sports they loved. They faced obstacles that my players couldn't even imagine, including an organized effort to shut down all women's competitive sports. Not too long ago, a statement I made about the need for more visible female role models went viral. I believe women's basketball teams should have female coaches so their players have someone who looks like them teaching them how to be leaders. But I also believe girls need to know about the trailblazers who came before them, whose determination made possible the opportunities they have today.

In sports and in life, you've got to learn from your defeats, but you've also got to celebrate your victories. *Breaking Through* celebrates the victories of some amazing female athletes. My players and all girls and women who play sports today should be inspired by their struggles and triumphs.

"Winning isn't really the point. Competing and giving it your best shot, that's the point. Learning the value of a great work ethic, and never giving up—that's the point."

—Muffet McGraw, "Want Your Kids To Thrive? Let Them Fail," CNN.com, December 20, 2018

Muffet McGraw (in print skirt) coaches the Notre Dame Fighting Irish in the 2019 NCAA Finals against Baylor.

INTRODUCTION

— SUE MACY —

As a kid in the early 1960s, I used to watch a TV series called *The Roaring 20's*. This drama was about gangsters and bootleggers and a lot of sketchy activity in, as the theme song said, "the wild and reckless, never boring ... soaring Roaring 20's." The women wore shimmering outfits and cloche hats and spoke in breathless tones. Sometimes they also sang, but they were strictly supporting players, at the beck and call of the men who drove the action.

Women are the main characters in *this* account of the Roaring Twenties. They wear swimsuits and soccer uniforms and carry tennis rackets and hockey sticks. The action revolves around them as they negotiate living in an era radically different from that of their grandmothers, or even their mothers. For starters, those in the United States had won the right to vote when the 19th Amendment to the Constitution became law on August 18, 1920. Many also had modern conveniences that improved everyday life and automobiles to travel beyond hearth and home whenever they desired.

And they had sports. The 1920s were considered the first golden age of sports, when athletic heroes were larger than life and spectators gathered en masse to cheer them on. Among those heroes were women who ran, swam, shot baskets, hit balls, and flew airplanes. The era was less golden for some of these women; most athletes of color had no choice but to compete in segregated leagues. But for the first time in history, female athletes were regularly drawing crowds and making headlines. In a list of standout sports stars of the decade, Gertrude Ederle and Isadore "Izzy" Channels are right up there with Babe Ruth and Jim Thorpe.

Just as the bicycle gave women freedom of movement in the 1890s and the automobile allowed them to drive boldly into the 20th century, sports in

"Nothing in the world more strikingly marks the great gap between the girl of today and her grandmother than that girl's place in the world of sport."

—"How Weak Is the Weaker Sex?"
The Woman Citizen, September 1925

the 1920s helped them redefine what it meant to be female. Suddenly women were displaying their strength and speed and courage and competitive spirit for all to see. They were proud of their accomplishments and enjoyed a new kind of sisterhood with teammates and opponents. But as women competed, social critics debated whether they had gone too far. Were their muscles too big? Their uniforms too small? Their attitudes too bold? Their ambitions too great?

Breaking Through looks at the female athletes who broadened the definition of femininity in the 1920s, as well as the critics who were unsettled by their success. The achievements of these athletes provided a foundation for the revolution in women's sports that would unfold as the 20th century progressed and for the expanding role of women in the world at large. It turns out the female protagonists of the "wild and reckless" Roaring Twenties were a lot more formidable than my childhood TV show ever suggested.

The author in her most triumphant athletic moment, earning a medal for finishing the 2005 Danskin Triathlon at Sandy Hook, New Jersey.

"Ancient ideas of women received a severe jolt when the campaign for suffrage got in full swing ... and suffered a knockout blow after the war with the entrance of girls and young women into the field of sports to an extent unprecedented in the history of the world."

—"Superwomen in Sports Developed in Decade," *New York Herald*, May 29, 1921

Aileen Riggin, shown here at an exhibition in 1922, took up diving after surviving the influenza epidemic of 1918–19.

CHAPTER 1

TAKING THE PLUNGE

— 1920–21 (AND BEFORE) —

Aileen Riggin shivered as she stared into the ominous water of the Olympic diving venue. It was so black that she feared she would be lost forever if she dove too deep and was sucked into the muddy bottom. Riggin and her teammates had hoped they'd be competing in a pristine 50-meter swimming pool at the 1920 Olympics. Unfortunately Belgium, the host country, was still recovering from World War I, which had devastated much of Europe between 1914 and 1918. Because the Belgians didn't have the resources to build a pool, all the divers and swimmers were sharing the icy Antwerp city moat.

Riggin, only 14 years old and weighing 65 pounds, stood anxiously on the plank of wood that had been set on springs for the first ever women's Olympic springboard diving competition.

Riggin performs a graceful dive into the less-than-inviting waters of the 1920 Olympic swimming and diving venue in Antwerp, Belgium.

She had completed her six required and four optional dives, as well as one of the two extra dives the judges had added to the program. She also had watched all her opponents do face-plants on the 12th and final dive, a running front somersault. When it was her turn, Riggin took her time, striding down the board carefully, deliberately. Then she pushed off and up, flipped over, and entered the water cleanly, feet first. She was supremely satisfied. After the dive, she and her teammates went for lunch at the Young Women's Christian Association (YWCA) Hostess House in Antwerp, where they were staying. Meanwhile, the judges did the math. "There were no computers," Riggin would remember decades later. "When they judged the diving, it was all by hand ... It took forever to find out who had won." Eventually, an official arrived to congratulate Riggin, the youngest member of the entire 1920 United States Olympic team. She had captured the gold.

Back home in New York City, Riggin's mother, Ella, celebrated. It had been a month of triumphs. On August 18, Ella Riggin had rejoiced when women's suffrage officially became the law of the land. She had worked passionately for the cause, stuffing envelopes and marching and putting up with whistles and catcalls from those who opposed giving women the vote. Now, just 11 days after that victory, she cheered her daughter's gold medal.

"Women as a class cannot stand a prolonged mental or physical strain as well as men. Exact it of them and they will try to do the work, but they will do it at a fearful cost to themselves and eventually to their children."

—Dudley A. Sargent, M.D., *Ladies' Home Journal*, March 1912

"She got both of her things that summer," remembered Riggin, and indeed, both of those successes signaled the start of a new era for American women. Before the 19th Amendment, only about seven million women could vote in the 21 states that had granted them that right. After the amendment, 27 million could go to the polls in every state of the Union.

Although it was a more modest achievement than women's suffrage, Aileen Riggin's gold medal also represented a significant leap forward for American women. No female athletes from the U.S. had competed in the first Olympic women's swimming and diving contests at the previous Summer Games in 1912. According to the *New York Times*, the American Olympic Committee, swayed by its powerful secretary, James E. Sullivan, "was opposed to women taking part in any event in which they could not wear long skirts." Sullivan saw the form-fitting bathing suits that competitive swimmers and divers wore as an affront to the modesty he admired in respectable women. And his disapproval had a great impact. Besides working with the Olympic Committee, Sullivan was a leader of the Amateur Athletic Union (AAU), the group that oversaw amateur sports in the U.S. At least one writer called him "the dictator of amateur athletics in this country."

Women's rights activist Alice Paul unfurls a suffrage flag from the balcony of the National Woman's Party headquarters in Washington, D.C., in 1920.

CRITIC

JAMES E. SULLIVAN

When James E. Sullivan died suddenly at age 52, the *New York Times* called him "America's Foremost Leader in Athletics and Recreation Work." Sullivan was an important figure in the early history of the Amateur Athletic Union and the Olympic movement, but he courted his share of controversy. Born in New York City, the onetime publisher of the newspaper the *Athletics News* was the principal organizer of the 1904 Olympic Games in St. Louis, Missouri. At those games, Sullivan dictated that there be only two water stations on the marathon course—then 24.85 miles instead of the current 26 miles 385 yards. He thought that denying the participants water in the 90-degree heat would allow doctors to conduct research on "purposeful dehydration." Not surprisingly, only 14 of the 32 runners finished the race.

Later in his career, Sullivan began to voice his opposition to female athletes. Only months before his death in 1914, he spearheaded a resolution declaring that the AAU's rules were "formed to include none but the male sex," effectively barring women from their competitions. Ironically, female athletes have always been eligible for the James E. Sullivan Award, given in his memory every year since 1930 to the most outstanding amateur athlete in the U.S. From its inception through 2017, 68 men and 22 women have won the award.

Note: There were two Sullivan Award winners in 1999 and 2015.

There's no doubt that Sullivan would have continued to block the participation of women in swimming and other sports had he not died unexpectedly on September 16, 1914, after surgery for intestinal trouble. His successors were more concerned with regulating women's sports than censoring them, and change came quickly. In November, the Amateur Athletic Union sanctioned its first women's events—in swimming, the very sport that had so offended Sullivan. The following year, swimmers and divers from New York and Philadelphia competed in the first women's AAU championships ever held. By July 1916, the *New York Times* felt confident in declaring, "Our women swimmers are rapidly advancing toward international leadership ... It will not be long before they brook no rivals." Unfortunately, they had to wait a bit longer when the 1916 Olympics were canceled because of World War I.

B**y the time Aileen Riggin** won her Olympic gold medal at the 1920 games, women in the U.S. had been enjoying sports and physical activity for more than half a century. But during most of that time, no one was trumpeting their talent or success. In the mid-1800s, some doctors and educators thought vigorous exercise would harm a woman's health, especially her ability to have children. Even Vassar, the first women's college to add physical education to its curriculum, warned its students about exercising during their monthly periods. "At the beginning of every collegiate year the students are carefully instructed regarding the precautions which are periodically necessary," wrote Alida C. Avery, Vassar's professor of physiology and hygiene, in 1873. "They are positively forbidden to take gymnastics at all during the first two days of their period ... They are also forbidden to ride on horseback then; and moreover, are strongly advised not to dance, nor *run* up and down stairs, nor do any thing else that gives sudden and successive (even though not violent) shocks to the trunk."

Besides offering opinions on the impact of exercise on women's health, late 19th-century scholars also debated the effects that a population of

Vassar students formed a baseball club in 1866, and it grew to feature as many as seven teams before it was discontinued in 1877. Here, the 1876 Vassar Resolutes gather for a team picture.

Female cyclists frequently graced the labels of cigar boxes like this one in the 1890s. The women often were shown in masculine garb, reflecting the blurring of gender roles as they embraced athletic pursuits.

exercise-loving women would have on society. In 1899, Arabella Kenealy, a British physician, wrote a controversial article that focused on a woman named Clara who had been rather placid until she discovered the freedom of bicycling. "When Clara tired with a walk beyond two miles," Kenealy wrote, "Clara took flowers and books to her sick or less fortunate friends. Now that she can 'manage twenty miles easily,' her sick and less fortunate friends miss her." Kenealy worried that Clara had embraced her new athletic powers at the expense of her responsibility as a nurturer. When her brother needed help with his lessons or her father's temper needed to be soothed, Clara had always been there, wrote Kenealy. But now she was riding her bicycle instead. A woman, Kenealy explained, is "a moral and refining influence; as sister, wife, or friend, an inspiration, a comrade and a comforter; as mother, a guardian and guide; as citizen or worker, a smoother of life's way, a humanizer, nurse, and teacher. But none of these, her highest attributes, are attributes of muscle!"

TRAILBLAZER

— IDA SCHNALL —

Few women in the early 20th century were more athletic than Ida Schnall. A Jewish immigrant from Tarnów, Austria, Schnall won prizes in swimming, diving, track and field, tennis, golf, basketball, ice-skating, and cycling, among other sports. And when doors were closed to her, she spoke up. After the American Olympic Committee decided not to send female swimmers or divers to the 1912 games, she repeatedly telephoned the powerful official James E. Sullivan to complain. Finally, she wrote a letter to the *New York Times,* claiming Sullivan was stuck in the past. "It's the athletic girl that takes the front seat today," she wrote, "and no one can deny it."

As if to prove her point, Schnall staked her claim to the national pastime. In 1913, she founded and pitched for the New York Female Giants, a women's baseball squad whose members played exhibition games against each other.

Then she took a detour to Hollywood, swimming and diving as a water nymph in the title role of the film *Undine*.

By 1921, Schnall was married and raising a family. Newspapers called her "The Most Athletic Mother on Earth," describing her as a sports champion "who finds ample time to bring up her two children and also to win prizes for darning socks." She preached the benefits of exercise for wives and mothers and continued to accept athletic challenges. That November, a newspaper reported Schnall thrilled crowds by diving into the ocean from the wing of an airplane, then rushed home to make curried chicken for her husband's dinner. Ida Schnall died on February 14, 1973, at age 83.

Ida Schnall proudly displays some of her trophies and medals.

Reprinted from the
***Star Press* (Muncie, Indiana)**

FEBRUARY 29, 1920

Woman Athlete Swings on Jaw of Burglar

LOS ANGELES, CAL., FEB. 28—Mrs. J. B. Statler is athletic. She is one of the star members of a woman's class at the athletic club and long has been regarded as a remarkably clever amateur boxer.

Recently she encountered a burglar in her home. Instead of running from the house, screaming for the police, she took the situation in her own hands. "Mr. Burglar, you may put up your hands and get ready for what probably will be the very worst licking you ever had." With the warning she stepped in with lightning right and left swings to the head. The burglar was groggy in a few seconds. He tried ineffectively to guard against the rain of blows. Finally with a wicked uppercut to the point of the jaw, Mrs. Statler knocked out the burglar.

He had not come to when the police loaded him in a patrol wagon and took him to a police station. ★

"It has become evident that the value of exercise as a remedial measure, cannot be overestimated, the lack of proper exercise often being at the root of depleted conditions of health."

—Lillian Curtis Drew, *American Physical Education Review*, June 1921

Though critics disagreed about the social implications of physical activity for women, most came to admit that engaging in exercise made women healthier. By the 1880s, girls at private schools and colleges were swimming, ice-skating, riding horses, and doing calisthenics and gymnastics. Women at country clubs were competing in archery tournaments and playing golf, tennis, and croquet. A few female daredevils even took up bicycle racing, riding "ordinary" bicycles—with very large front wheels and very small rear wheels—for hours on end around a banked track. Female pedestrians competed in walking marathons against the clock or each other. But all that was prelude to an explosion of sports opportunities for women and girls in the 1890s and early 1900s.

That explosion began with the safety bicycle. Unlike the unstable ordinary, the safety had two wheels of equal or almost equal diameter and cushiony pneumatic tires. Cycling on a safety appealed to women, offering them both physical exercise and a chance for independence that was impossible to resist. Though some medical professionals voiced concerns about excessive bicycle riding—especially

Senda Berenson (in long skirt) teaches the basics of basketball. At Smith College's earliest games, students tossed the ball into wastepaper baskets hung from the ceiling.

during pregnancy—women across economic and racial lines started cycling for fun and sport in the 1890s.

At the same time, Senda Berenson, a physical education instructor at Smith College, added a new activity to her curriculum. Basketball had just been invented down the road in Springfield, Massachusetts, as an indoor game to keep boys busy during the cold New England winter. Berenson thought it would perk up her classes and help her female students develop teamwork. She rewrote the rules for women, aiming to create a less strenuous game by outlawing stealing and assigning players to stay in a specific third of the court. Basketball quickly spread to other schools. Soon businesses started company teams for female employees, and YWCAs and churches in both white and black communities formed women's leagues.

Suddenly females weren't just performing repetitive exercises; they were competing. Volleyball joined the mix soon afterward, followed by field hockey, which

"The Women's Sports Page of <u>The Sunday Beacon</u> is a hummer. I did not think there would be enough material for such a department, but see now there is plenty if one will go after it."

—R. A. Clymer, Editor of the *Eldorado Times* in the *Wichita* (Kansas) *Beacon*, December 19, 1920

Multisport athlete Ida Schnall winds up to deliver a pitch for the New York Female Giants baseball team in 1913.

was introduced to U.S. women's colleges in 1901. But the transition from exercise to competitive sports made critics nervous. "Some people advocate girls' athletics without competition, that their aim should be merely to work to surpass one's own record," wrote Florence A. Somers in 1916. "It would be extremely difficult to interest the majority of girls over fourteen in athletic sports without the spirit of competition." Even so Somers, who would go on to be a leader in women's sports, said it was important not to overemphasize winning "so much that the girl thinks more of the competition than of the game." Others warned of following the lead of men's teams by playing for their fans' admiration instead of their own fulfillment and focusing on publicity and gate receipts.

Despite these apprehensions, the prospects for athletically inclined women were looking good by 1920. A study that year showed almost every state required physical education for all high school students, male and female. What's more, 22 percent of the universities in the U.S. offered at least one women's intercollegiate team. Reports on women's events started to show up on the sports pages, and Aileen Riggin and other female athletes reached celebrity status. In December 1920, one newspaper, the *Wichita* (Kansas) *Beacon*, added a full page of women's sports news every Sunday, to the delight of its readers.

Yet an incident the following year revealed an underlying discomfort with the growing triumphs of women in sports. In November 1921, an official from the Syracuse University men's baseball squad reached out to schedule a game with a college he'd been told had an outstanding team. He didn't know that the school, Goucher, was a women's college. Rather than expressing respect for the Goucher team, newspapers nationwide reported the mistake as "the big joke of the year in college circles." In the decade ahead, critics often would react to advances made by female athletes with sarcasm or ridicule. The more success women in sports achieved, the more threatening they would become to those who held tightly to society's accepted gender roles.

Reprinted from the *Houston* (Texas) *Post*

NOVEMBER 4, 1921

Bob-O-Link Club Bars Women From Links

CHICAGO, NOV. 3—Action by the Bob-o'-Link Golf club in barring women from its links is not spreading to other golf clubs. In fact, women have started such a campaign that it would be exceedingly risky to even suggest forbidding them to play at other clubs. Bob-o'-Link formulated its rule, put it over and got away clean before there was any opportunity for a fight, but the others are hastening to give assurances that the farthest thing from their minds is the barring of women.

"The women are just as important as the men at our club," said Miss Gloria Chandler, head of the women's golf activities at Glen View. "Of course we never try to play on holidays or Saturday afternoons until after 3 o'clock, but there isn't a man in the club who ever considered excluding us."

"The women—God bless 'em!" said Fred H. Burnabee, one of the club's most ardent golfers and vice chairman of the 1921 tournament, "will never be barred from Westmoreland." ★

ALSO IN 1920–21

Women's athletic achievements in the Roaring Twenties took place in a world that had changed drastically over just a few years. More than 15 million people had lost their lives during World War I, from 1914 through 1918, and at least 50 million more had died in the influenza (flu) pandemic of 1918 and 1919. Many Americans sought to escape the trauma of those events by isolating themselves from global concerns. Some developed a fear of foreigners and a distrust of people with radical political views. Meanwhile, black citizens, 85 percent of whom lived in the South in 1920, had begun a Great Migration to northern cities, seeking new economic opportunities and an escape from racist laws and violence. Here are some developments that helped shape the nation in 1920 and 1921.

1920

✷ ACLU ESTABLISHED

JANUARY 1920: Jane Addams, Jeannette Rankin, and Helen Keller are among the social reformers who organize the American Civil Liberties Union (ACLU). The group declares its intention to fight legal battles against all attempts to violate the rights of free speech, freedom of the press, and peaceful assembly guaranteed in the Bill of Rights of the U.S. Constitution. The ACLU also pledges to combat racial discrimination and defend the rights of immigrants. Its platform is in part a response to the crackdown on radicals and suspected Communists in the U.S. following World War I.

A New York restaurant displays its policy during Prohibition.

✷ PROHIBITION

JANUARY 17, 1920: The 18th Amendment to the U.S. Constitution takes effect, prohibiting the production, transport, and sale of intoxicating liquor, including beer and wine. The result of a decades-long campaign by religious and women's groups, prohibition quickly backfires as ordinary citizens willingly break the law to take a drink. Organized crime starts smuggling liquor into the country from Mexico and Canada, and individuals brew their own "bathtub gin" at home. Speakeasies—establishments that sell illegal liquor—make a lot of money for their criminal owners, who bribe officials to let them operate. By the early 1930s, popular opinion would turn against Prohibition. It would be repealed by the 21st Amendment in 1933.

Jeannette Rankin during her campaign for Congress in 1916

✷ FIRST BLACK BASEBALL LEAGUE

FEBRUARY 13, 1920: Andrew "Rube" Foster, an outstanding pitcher and manager, organizes the Negro National League, the first professional baseball league for black athletes. Though major league teams had fielded a handful of black players in the 1800s, that practice stopped when racist owners, egged on by a few bigoted stars, refused to play against them. In response, black players formed their own teams and barnstormed across the country. However, their appearances were overseen by white booking agents, who took a big cut of the profits. In Foster's league, black men would control their own destiny. The Negro National League would fold in 1932, but other "Negro leagues" would continue through the 1950s, when the major leagues finally were integrated.

Andrew "Rube" Foster

✷ FOREIGNERS EXECUTED

JULY 14, 1921: Despite a defense team provided by the ACLU, two Italian immigrants, Nicola Sacco and Bartolomeo Vanzetti, are convicted on sparse evidence of murdering two men during the robbery of a shoe factory in Massachusetts. Protesters, including writers, artists, and future Supreme Court Justice Felix Frankfurter, would charge that the men were railroaded because of xenophobia, the fear of foreigners or those who are different. These protesters would claim the foreign birth and radical political views of the two defendants prompted the judge and jury to presume their guilt. In fact, both men would continue to profess their innocence throughout a series of appeals. In the end, the verdict would be upheld, and Sacco and Vanzetti would be executed on August 23, 1927.

Nicola Sacco

Bartolomeo Vanzetti

1921

✷ FIRST LICENSED RADIO STATION

NOVEMBER 2, 1920: The first licensed radio station, KDKA in Pittsburgh, Pennsylvania, makes what is considered the first radio broadcast when it announces Warren Harding's victory in the presidential election. It wouldn't take long for radio to transform how news and entertainment were delivered across the country. As the sale of radio receivers soared, the number of licensed stations would grow, reaching 556 by 1923. Soon networks of affiliated stations would share programming and broadcast the news—and sports—as it happened.

Anna Chow (left) and Lilly Chow of San Francisco listen to the radio in 1922.

Margaret Gorman

✷ FIRST MISS AMERICA

SEPTEMBER 7–8, 1921: In order to extend their peak season beyond Labor Day, business owners in the beach town of Atlantic City, New Jersey, hold their first "Inter-City Beauty" contest. Thousands of spectators watch women in one-piece bathing suits parade along the beach, scandalizing some with their bare arms and legs. Sixteen-year-old Margaret Gorman, "Miss Washington, D.C.," is crowned the "Golden Mermaid"—later renamed "Miss America." Throughout its history, the Miss America pageant would wrestle with criticism that it judged women on their looks rather than their skills. In 2018, the pageant would finally abandon its swimsuit competition and focus on contestants' talents and answers to interview questions instead.

"We play for the love of the game and we are determined to carry on."

—Alice Kell, captain of the Dick, Kerr Ladies, *Lancashire* (England) *Daily Post*, December 1921

Jennie Harris (above) was a prodigious scorer and one of the original members of the Dick, Kerr Ladies football team.

CHAPTER 2

CREATING OPPORTUNITIES

— 1922–23 —

When Alice Kell and her teammates set sail for North America in 1922, it was as if their athletic lives depended on it. Kell was the captain of the Dick, Kerr Ladies football (soccer) team of Preston, England. The team, named after the manufacturing company that sponsored it, had been formed in 1917 to raise money for wartime charities. In five years, it had donated tens of thousands of British pounds from ticket sales to help wounded soldiers and unemployed veterans. The Dick, Kerr Ladies regularly drew crowds of 10,000 or more to their matches, and in 1920 they played the first international women's soccer tournament on record, against a team from France. But on December 5, 1921, England's Football Association (FA) passed a resolution.

It stated that “the game of football is quite unsuitable for females and ought not to be encouraged.” The FA banned all women’s teams from playing on any soccer pitch owned by its clubs.

Special lighting was erected at the Burnley Cricket Club in Lancashire, England, when the Dick, Kerr Ladies (in striped jerseys) played the Heys of Bradford (in white jerseys) in the 1924 match illustrated here.

“They certainly rule English football,” said Kell, “but not the world, thank goodness.” Instead of letting the FA’s ban derail them, the Dick, Kerr Ladies traveled across the Atlantic, where they hoped to play women’s teams in Canada and the United States. They were rebuffed by Canada; the governing body of Canadian soccer denied their request to play there, most likely at the urging of England’s FA. And although they were welcome to play in the United States, there were no women’s teams in the country with enough experience to challenge them. That’s how, less than a year after the idea of a men’s baseball team playing a women’s team was considered a joke, a women’s soccer team started a nine-game series against some of the top men’s soccer teams in the U.S.

Perhaps surprisingly, Dick, Kerr’s opponents, as well as the reporters who covered the matches, treated them with respect and a little awe. “The women kicked off and displayed expertness in the free, open style of play which

> **"Our girl athletes cannot expect a walkover victory at Paris. They can win only by superior merit. European women were mobilized for war for several years, and mobilization for sport will be correspondingly easier for them."**
>
> —Editorial Before the Women's Games, *Norwich* (Connecticut) *Bulletin*, August 5, 1922

distinguishes the English from the more aggressive and somewhat rougher Yankee tactics," wrote the *New York Times* on September 25, 1922. The paper cited Jennie Harris, whose "passing was splendid and the way she followed up would put many a veteran male to shame," and wrote of Lily Parr, "Her driving from the wing and the accuracy of her shots left little to be desired." When the Ladies departed the United States on November 9, they could hold their heads high. During their grueling tour, they had tallied three wins, three ties, and three losses against men's teams across the mid-Atlantic states and New England. They had given Americans a glimpse of soccer at its highest level, foreshadowing the emergence of the U.S. women's national team decades into the future. And they had shown that female athletes could be as tough and unforgiving as men, telling one reporter, "We give no quarter and ask none."

Alice Milliat credited her experience as a rower with giving her the courage and confidence to become a leader in the fight for more opportunities for female athletes.

Just weeks before the Dick, Kerr Ladies left for America, female athletes from the U.S., France, Switzerland, Czechoslovakia, and Great Britain descended on Paris, France, to strike a blow for gender equality at the Women's Olympic Games. The games took place at Pershing Stadium on a single day, August 20, 1922. Their goals were to showcase talented track-and-field stars and to protest the International Olympic Committee (IOC)'s refusal to add women's track events to the upcoming 1924 Olympics.

Alice Milliat, who had accompanied the French women's soccer team to England when they played the Dick, Kerr Ladies two years earlier, was the driving force behind the Women's Games. In 1921, Milliat had founded the Fédération Sportive Féminine Internationale (FSFI) to create opportunities for and regulate women's sports competitions. Milliat would hold her sports festival every four years through 1934, changing its name to the Women's World Games after the first edition because the IOC demanded that she remove the word "Olympics."

Close to 20,000 spectators witnessed the 1922 Women's Olympic Games. They saw 18 new women's world records set in 11 events. Great Britain led the field with five gold medals, just edging out the Americans, who won four. Twenty-year-old Camelia Sabie, of Newark, New Jersey, was the standout for the U.S., earning gold medals in the 100-yard hurdles and the standing broad jump, and a bronze medal in the running broad jump. After Sabie set a world record in the trials for the hurdles and then broke her own record in the finals, newspapers interviewed her proud Italian immigrant mother. "Ever since she was a little girl, she has been what you call a 'tomboy,'" Mrs. Sabie said. "Climbing trees or fences, or running with the boys, was more fun for her than playing with dolls." Sabie would compete in a few more track meets when she returned to Newark, but she rejected offers from Hollywood to display her athletic skills in the movies. Instead, she earned a degree in elementary education and got a job teaching school.

Explaining why she chose teaching over Hollywood, Camelia Sabie said, "I have my school, my children, my gymnasium class, my home, my mother and father. I couldn't have them in Hollywood. I'd rather be a school teacher in Newark than star in all the movies in the world!"

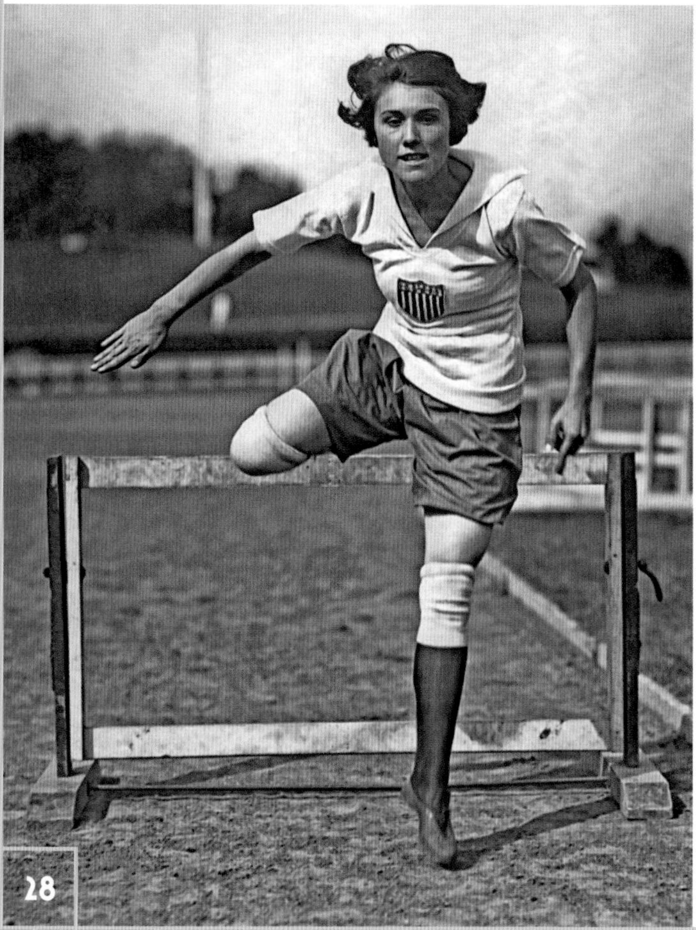

While Alice Milliat was fighting to expand opportunities in track and field for female athletes and the Dick, Kerr Ladies were demonstrating their passionate embrace of competition, a power struggle was being fought in the United States over the future direction of women's sports. On the eve of the 1922 Women's Olympic Games, leaders of the Amateur Athletic Union declared, "The time has come for properly regulating girls' athletics." The AAU intended to consult medical authorities and then standardize events and rules for women's track-and-field competitions. But female physical educators were appalled that an organization run by men would presume to know what was best for women, and they resolved to take control themselves. They had the perfect platform in a new organization, the National Amateur Athletic Federation (NAAF).

When the NAAF was formed in 1922, Lou Henry Hoover, the leader of the Girl Scouts of the United States, was named a vice president. Hoover, whose husband would become president of the United States in 1929, took it upon herself to create a Women's Division of the NAAF to advocate for girls. Hoover and her executive committee rejected the AAU's endorsement

CRITIC

LOU HENRY HOOVER

Lou Henry Hoover's biography does not paint the picture of a woman who shied away from competition. America's future first lady was adventurous and athletic and broke barriers at an early age, graduating from Stanford University in 1898 as the only female geology major in her class. In the 1920s, Hoover served as president and then chairperson of the board of directors of the Girl Scouts of the United States. Among the programs she instituted was one that encouraged Scouts' entrepreneurial spirit by having them bake and sell cookies (for 25 to 30 cents a dozen).

Yet today, Hoover is remembered as one of the people largely responsible for derailing interscholastic competition for female athletes in the 1920s and beyond. In its early meetings, her Women's Division went so far as to officially oppose the participation of women at the Olympic Games. The group's 1931 platform would condemn "the making and breaking of records and the winning of championships for the enjoyment of spectators and for the athletic reputation or commercial advantage of institutions and organizations." Though Hoover believed her policies would protect female athletes, they inadvertently implied that women were not tough enough for sports and other competitive endeavors. This, in turn, cast competitive women as "unnatural" or "manly," an impression that only started to change in the early years of the 21st century. Lou Henry Hoover died on January 7, 1944, at age 69.

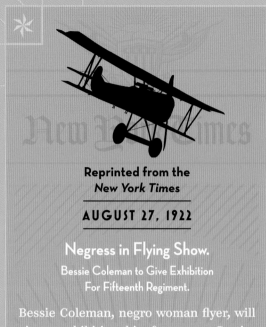

Reprinted from the *New York Times*

AUGUST 27, 1922

Negress in Flying Show.

Bessie Coleman to Give Exhibition For Fifteenth Regiment.

Bessie Coleman, negro woman flyer, will give an exhibition this afternoon at Curtiss Field, near Mineola, L.I. [Long Island], for the Fifteenth Regiment, which is expected to turn out in full strength. Miss Coleman returned from Europe a fortnight ago and, according to German newspapers, in June she flew, without a lesson, the largest plane ever piloted by a woman. She took a 400 horsepower machine over Berlin. She visited the Fokker plant in the Netherlands and successfully flew the various types manufactured by the Dutch aircraft engineer. Another feat ascribed to her was piloting a Dornier seaplane, which requires unusual aeronautical skill.

Miss Coleman, who is 24 years old, is a native of Texas. Just before the war closed she went to France with a Red Cross unit, which was brigaded with a French flying unit. She persuaded the French officers to instruct her and now possesses a pilot's license issued by the Fédération Aéronautique Internationale. ★

Note: This primary source article was printed verbatim. It includes the terms "Negress" and "negro," which are considered offensive today but were commonly used in 1922.

"It seems to me ... that unless a very definite stand is taken ... we will find ourselves fighting the same vicious system that the men are doing, and that our women will be having commercially sponsored athletics."

—Blanche Trilling in a letter to Lou Henry Hoover, February 2, 1923

of international competition for female athletes. They focused on providing fitness for the masses rather than on developing the superior abilities of a select few. They agreed that physical activity helped girls become fit and increased social skills, but felt that cut-throat, competitive sports contests were detrimental to girls' physical and mental health. "A sport for every girl and every girl in a sport" was the philosophy the Women's Division espoused. These leaders believed that the women of the 20th century should be vigorous and strong. But according to committee member J. Anna Norris, they drew the line at "the development of aggressive characteristics that ... were not in harmony with the best traditions of the [female] sex."

Aiming to help all girls and women achieve optimal health through sports, the Women's Division proposed play days rather than interscholastic competitions for girls in high school and college. When two or more schools met for a play day, educators randomly assigned students from different institutions to play together on teams. That negated the intense rivalries between schools in traditional sports programs and allowed every girl to take part and have fun. Play days typically also featured social hours, singing, folk dancing, and swimming or running events in which everyone could participate. If prizes were given, they were usually just inexpensive tokens of the day, such as tin cups with different colored bows. One account of a play day reflected the results Hoover was seeking. "Amid cheers and toasts for each college, the players made their departures in the same good spirit as their arrivals, glorified by a day of fun, many new acquaintances, and the happy satisfaction of competition with and against friends instead of the strain of intercollegiate competition."

By the end of the 1920s, policies supported by the physical educators in the Women's Division would lead to the dismantling of many interscholastic sports programs for girls. As a result, males and females would have vastly different opportunities in school sports for decades to come. But the situation was somewhat different in the black community.

Bessie Coleman was the first African-American woman as well as the first woman of Native American descent to earn a pilot's license. A successful air show pilot, she hoped to start a school for black aviators but died in a plane crash on April 30, 1926. She was 34 years old. (The article at left misstates her age. She was born January 26, 1892.)

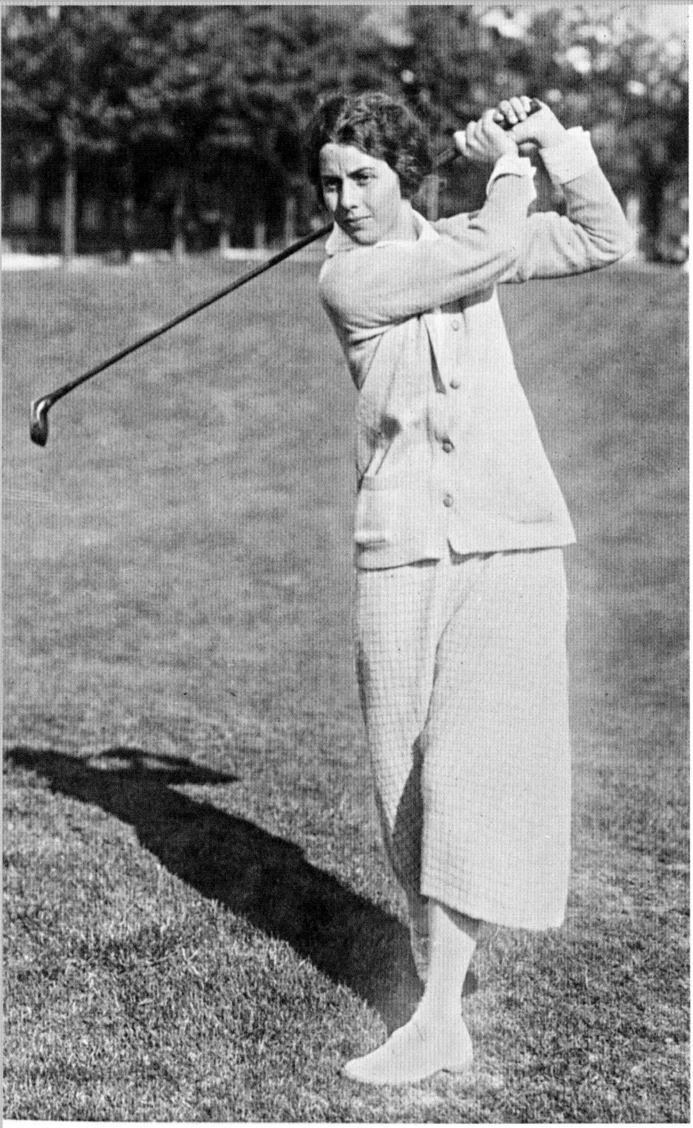

During her career, Glenna Collett would win six U.S. Women's Amateur Golf Championships. In 1924, she would win 59 of the 60 matches she played, losing only when her opponent's ball hit hers and fell into the hole during a playoff round.

At the time, laws in the United States segregated, or separated, blacks and whites in many aspects of their daily lives. This system resulted in lost opportunities for blacks and would not begin to change until the 1950s and 1960s. In education, black Americans founded a network of colleges and universities for students who were excluded from attending most other schools. These institutions celebrated strength and athleticism in women with enthusiasm not always seen at predominantly white schools. Even so, the National Association of College Women (NACW), which focused on improving higher education opportunities for black women, endorsed play days over more competitive women's sports programs. The impact of the Women's Division was hard to escape.

Sports outside the educational setting were beyond the reach of the Women's Division, however, and female athletes in competitive and even extreme sports continued to thrive. In 1922 alone, 19-year-old golfer Glenna Collett won her first U.S. amateur golf championship, kicking off a decade of dominating the game and the headlines. The Wimbledon singles final in England between U.S. national tennis champion Molla Bjurstedt Mallory and French star Suzanne Lenglen was front-page news. (Lenglen won, 6–2, 6–0.) And more than 1,000 people turned out to watch pioneering black aviator Bessie Coleman take practice flights on Long Island, New York.

— ISADORE "IZZY" CHANNELS —

For several years in the 1920s, Izzy Channels was the queen of the courts in both tennis and basketball. She won four national women's singles titles at the annual championships sponsored by the American Tennis Association (ATA) with her hard-hit, topspin shots. Although her achievements were rarely mentioned in the mainstream (white) press, black newspapers celebrated her athleticism. Pittsburgh's weekly black paper, the *Courier*, cited Channels' "smoking drives and uncanny volleying," and felt that, if given the chance, "Miss Channels would hold her own with the best [white] tournament players of the world."

Channels did compete against white athletes in basketball. She was a founding member of the Roamer Girls, a team in her adopted city of Chicago. Unlike most women's teams, Chicago squads used men's rules, with all players covering the whole court. Channels was often the Roamer Girls' high scorer. In a February 1925 win against the Harvey Bloomers, a squad of white players, Channels scored 19 of her team's 29 points. The *Chicago Defender* described her as "scoring and passing at will," and decided that "she played a game far above the heads of her opponents and far in advance of her colleagues."

Though she left high school as a teenager, Channels returned to school at age 24 and graduated at 26. As a student, she coached the tennis team. After graduation, she studied nursing, working in public health and then as a school nurse. But she kept her hand in sports. At age 40, she came in second in a golf tournament in St. Louis, Missouri. Izzy Channels died on June 30, 1959, at age 59.

Although Izzy Channels has long been a legend in sports history, the only known photographs of her exist in faded newspapers. Our illustrator drew this picture based on those photographs.

Reprinted from the *Press and Sun-Bulletin* (Binghamton, New York)

NOVEMBER 23, 1922

Girl Athlete Braves Censors of Scanty Garb

U. of W. Co-Ed Isn't Sorry She Posed in Men's Clothes

SEATTLE, WASH., NOV. 23—Miss Julia Durrant, sophomore at the University of Washington, is out of athletics at that institution for the rest of the quarter, it is officially reported, because a newspaper Sunday printed a photograph of her wearing running trunks like those worn by men track athletes.

Miss Julia Boone, Miss Velda Cundiff and Miss Katherine Bailey were called before a faculty committee with Miss Durrant, all having appeared in the same photograph and Miss Boone having been dressed just like Miss Durrant. It is said that all except Miss Durrant expressed contrition but she declared she was in a movement to broaden athletics for girls at the university and that she would fight it out to the end.

According to Miss Mary Gross, head of the university department of physical education for women, a jumper-bloomer suit of serge is the limit for girl athletes. ★

Also in 1922, Chicago's Isadore "Izzy" Channels captured her first singles title as well as the mixed doubles crown at the American Tennis Association's national championships. The ATA had been formed in 1916 to promote tennis in black communities and offer opportunities for competition. As a result of segregation, black men and women were barred from many public tennis courts, and the sport's national governing body, the United States Lawn Tennis Association, excluded black athletes from its clubs and tournaments. The leaders of the ATA planned to encourage the building of courts that welcomed all players. The group did not write language into its bylaws excluding whites because, according to historian Sundiata Djata, it hoped that "enlightened whites ultimately would play under its auspices for a genuine national championship." A few white players eventually did enter ATA tournaments. Black golfers faced similar discrimination, and in 1925 they would form the United Golf Association (UGA).

At the end of 1923, the landscape for women's sports in the United States was expanding, even as the debates about what was appropriate for female athletes intensified. Besides the physical educators in the Women's Division, others were beginning to express concerns about the impact of sports on a woman's femininity. "The muscular man is attractive.

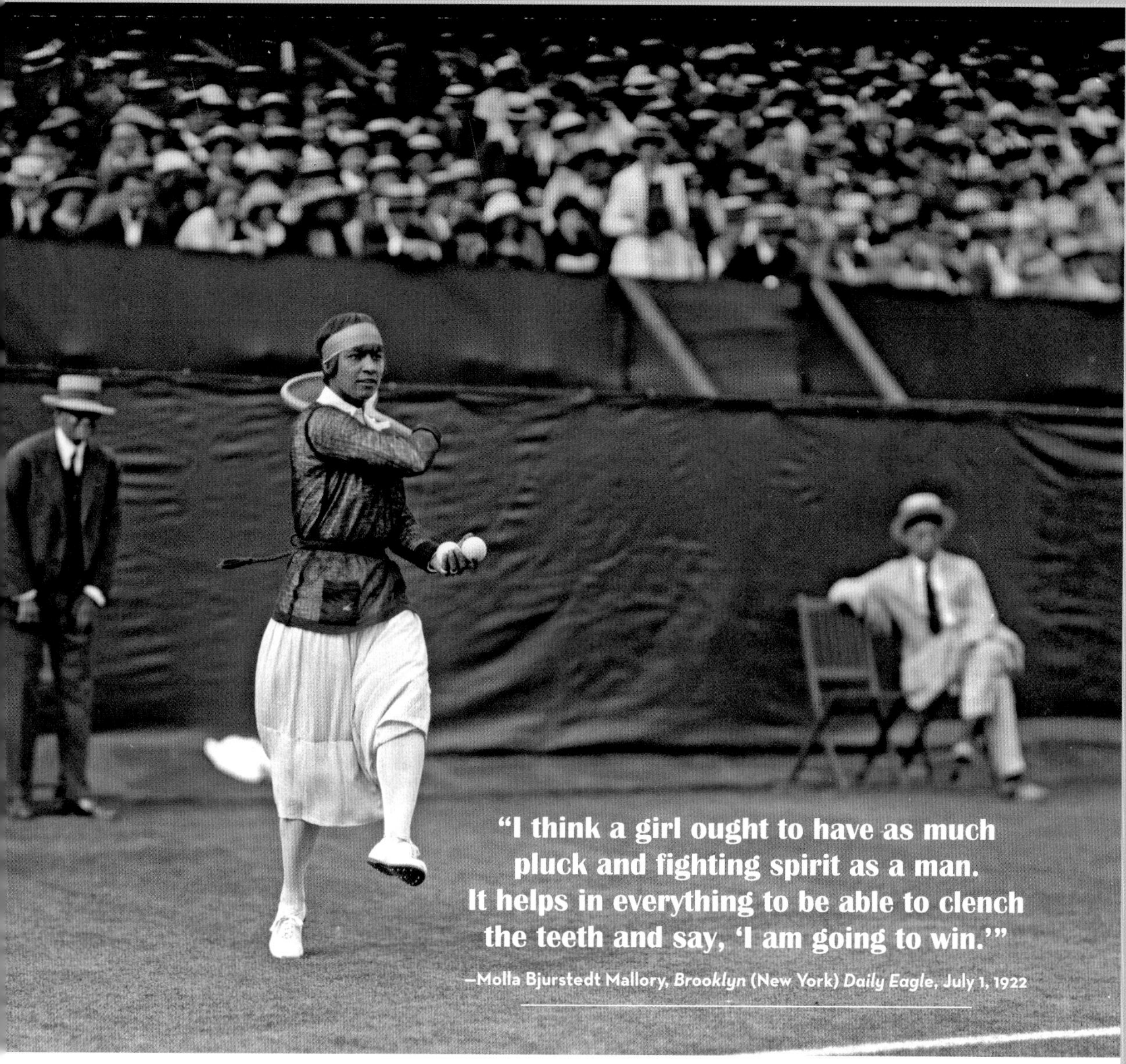

"I think a girl ought to have as much pluck and fighting spirit as a man. It helps in everything to be able to clench the teeth and say, 'I am going to win.'"
—Molla Bjurstedt Mallory, *Brooklyn* (New York) *Daily Eagle*, July 1, 1922

Molla Bjurstedt Mallory emigrated to the United States from Norway in 1915 and won the first of her eight U.S. Nationals singles titles that same year.

A muscular woman is ugly," declared Indiana Gyberson, a female painter. Gyberson, who often painted portraits of women, felt that swimmers were the only female athletes with "a beautiful form." Meanwhile Arthur Jacobson, a medical doctor and journalist from Brooklyn, New York, worried in print about the "severe violence being done to the delicate organism of growing girls and mature women" who played sports. To Gyberson and Jacobson, muscles, sweat, and intense physical effort were inconsistent with femininity. As the decade progressed, this preoccupation with femininity would increasingly show up in articles about women's athletic achievements.

ALSO IN 1922–23

While the debate about women's athletic participation began to take shape in 1922 and 1923, political scandals rocked the nation. Things came to a head in April 1922, when President Harding's secretary of the interior was accused of accepting bribes in awarding drilling rights at Wyoming's Teapot Dome oil reserves. Just four months later, Harding died of a heart attack. Teapot Dome and Harding's death left Americans disillusioned with government, contributing to the freewheeling mood of an untethered population. As ambitious social initiatives stalled in Congress, many people focused on fun and frivolity. But there were some important innovations as well. Here are some noteworthy developments from 1922 and 1923.

1922

✱ INSULIN FOR DIABETES

JANUARY 11, 1922: The health prospects for millions of people improve when two Canadians, Dr. Frederick Banting and his assistant, Charles Best, along with Scottish biochemist J. J. R. Macleod, establish insulin as a drug to treat diabetes by injecting their first patient, a 14-year-old boy named Leonard Thompson. A hormone produced by the pancreas, insulin helps the body absorb carbohydrates. It would become the go-to treatment for managing diabetes, saving an estimated 25 million lives in the next 50 years. Thompson, who had been near death, would continue taking insulin and live until age 27 before dying of pneumonia. Banting and Macleod would win the 1923 Nobel Prize in physiology or medicine.

Canadian stamp honoring the discovery of insulin

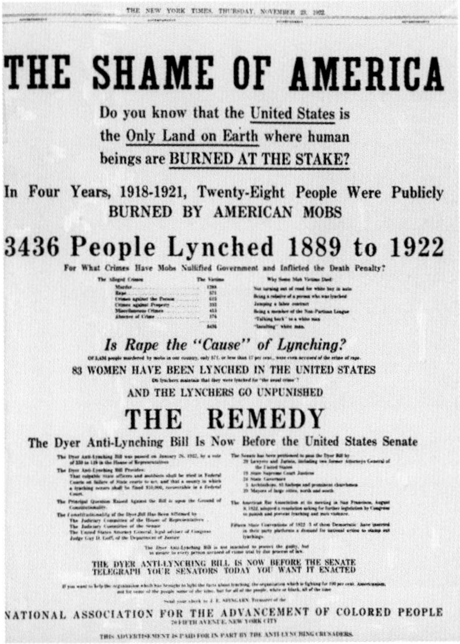

THE NEW YORK TIMES, THURSDAY, NOVEMBER 23, 1922

THE SHAME OF AMERICA

Do you know that the United States is the Only Land on Earth where human beings are BURNED AT THE STAKE?

In Four Years, 1918-1921, Twenty-Eight People Were Publicly BURNED BY AMERICAN MOBS

3436 People Lynched 1889 to 1922

For What Crimes Have Mobs Nullified Government and Inflicted the Death Penalty?

Is Rape the "Cause" of Lynching?

83 WOMEN HAVE BEEN LYNCHED IN THE UNITED STATES

AND THE LYNCHERS GO UNPUNISHED

THE REMEDY

The Dyer Anti-Lynching Bill Is Now Before the United States Senate

THE DYER ANTI-LYNCHING BILL IS NOW BEFORE THE SENATE
TELEGRAPH YOUR SENATORS TODAY YOU WANT IT ENACTED

NATIONAL ASSOCIATION FOR THE ADVANCEMENT OF COLORED PEOPLE

✱ AGAINST LYNCHING

JANUARY 26, 1922: After a campaign by civil rights groups, the U.S. House of Representatives passes a bill to make lynching a federal felony. Lynching, murders—especially by hanging—frequently committed by white mobs to keep blacks "in their place," often went unpunished. President Harding supports the bill, but segregationists in the Senate filibuster to keep it from coming to a vote so it never becomes law. Although the publicity surrounding the bill would lead to an outcry against lynching, the U.S. Senate would not pass an anti-lynching bill until 2018. That bill, which would make it a federal hate crime when two or more people injured or killed someone because of race, color, religion, or national origin, was awaiting a vote in the House when this book went to press.

Advertisement from the NAACP raising awareness about lynching, 1922

✷ EMILY POST'S *ETIQUETTE*

JULY 1922: Emily Price Post, a successful writer of novels and magazine articles, publishes *Etiquette in Society, in Business, in Politics, and at Home,* an advice book outlining proper behavior for men and women in all sorts of situations. Post's pronouncements are based on lessons learned during her elite upbringing, including her attendance at a finishing school, where upper-class students are taught the social graces. Post claims that her aim is to create not "a fellowship of the wealthy" but "an association of gentle-folk." Despite the tendency toward rebelliousness in the 1920s, *Etiquette* is a best seller. With frequent updates, the book would serve as a guide to manners for much of the 20th century.

Emily Post

✷ EQUAL RIGHTS

JANUARY 8, 1923: Having achieved their goal of a constitutional amendment granting women the right to vote, the National Woman's Party launches a campaign for passage of an Equal Rights Amendment (ERA) to the Constitution. Under the leadership of Alice Paul, the party seeks full equality with men. Other feminists oppose the ERA, worrying that it would jeopardize protections working women already had won. The debate would extend into the 1970s, when Congress would approve the ERA and 35 of the required 38 states would ratify it. Though its progress would stall and the original deadline for ratification would pass, a 36th state (Nevada) would ratify the ERA in 2017 and a 37th (Illinois) in 2018, leaving it one state short of becoming law when this book went to press.

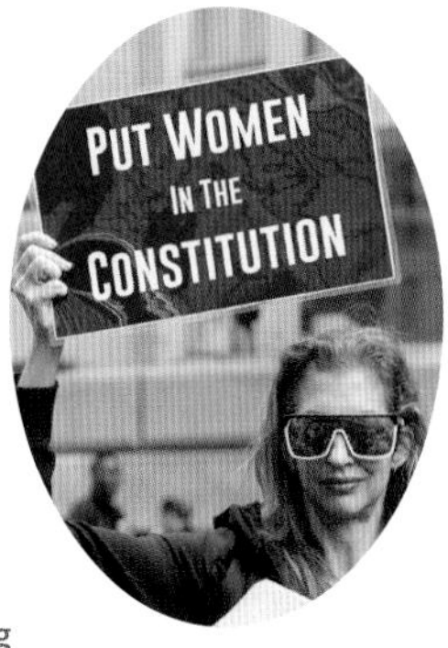

Marching for the ERA in 2018

1923

✷ FABULOUS FADS

1922–23: Americans don't just embrace sports in the 1920s. They also go crazy for fads. After centuries of wearing their hair long, many women flock to barber shops for bob haircuts, getting their tresses cropped straight around the head, usually at jaw level. First worn by female war workers during World War I, the bob becomes a symbol of liberation for women in the Roaring Twenties. Meanwhile, a British archaeologist finds the nearly intact tomb of Egypt's boy pharaoh Tutankhamun in November 1922, and people become fascinated with ancient Egypt. Soon "King Tut" merchandise is selling like hotcakes. And in 1923, the dance marathon is born when a woman named Alma Cummings dances for 27 continuous hours with six different partners. It's not long before couples are pushing the limit, dancing for days, and sometimes weeks, in pursuit of cash prizes.

Tutankhamun's funeral mask on display in 2014

A flapper trades her tired partner for a fresh one while dancing the Charleston.

✷ THE CHARLESTON

OCTOBER 29, 1923: *Runnin' Wild,* an all-black musical, opens on Broadway and includes "The Charleston," a song by composer James P. Johnson inspired by a beat he first heard in Charleston, South Carolina. The energetic dance steps that accompany the song recall moves that date back centuries in Africa. Already familiar to black audiences, now they are a hit with white Americans, who eagerly embrace black innovations in music and dance even as they discriminate against black people in everyday life. Soon the Charleston is all the rage at speakeasies, at dance marathons, and in the movies, and composers write new songs to keep people on their feet. Before long the Charleston becomes the signature dance of the Roaring Twenties.

“The hard-hitting girl athlete is giving men a new respect for women and women a revelation concerning themselves.”

—Editorial, *Boston Globe*, March 19, 1925

Two field hockey players take part in a bully to start a game. This method of beginning play would be discontinued in 1981.

CHAPTER 3

GAINING RECOGNITION

— 1924–25 —

Constance Applebee was not impressed when she learned what the coursework for women would include at her Harvard summer school class on indoor track. Born in England, Applebee was a graduate of the British College of Physical Education and had come to Massachusetts to further her training. But she scoffed upon seeing "musical chairs" in the women's curriculum. "We play those games at parties," she said. "For exercise we play hockey." Applebee proceeded to round up 22 women, a ball, and an armload of long sticks. Then, right smack in the middle of storied Harvard Yard, she gave her first American tutorial on the British game of field hockey.

"That famous sport-exhilarated American public has been worshipping too long at the shrine of our Bill Tildens and Bobby Joneses ... It's time to call for a new deal and give a few 'cheerios' to these sterling women athletes, such as Helen Wills, Glenna Collett and Gertrude Ederle."

—*Daily News* (New York, New York), September 27, 1925

That was in 1901. Over the next two decades "the Apple," as she came to be known, demonstrated field hockey at all the major women's colleges in the United States, and settled in as director of physical education at Bryn Mawr in Pennsylvania. In 1922, she co-founded the United States Field Hockey Association, an organization she would lead for 20 years. She also started a three-week intensive field hockey camp that would thrive for much of the 20th century. By 1924, the Apple was ready for a new challenge, one that would consolidate the ideas and concerns of

Constance Applebee, shown here demonstrating field hockey circa 1903, would also help to establish lacrosse as a women's sport in the United States. She would live to be 107 years old.

female athletes across the country. In September of that year, she launched *The Sportswoman*. It was, she explained in the first issue, "a woman's magazine, published by women, devoted to all forms of sports in which women take part, linking together the interests of all players and keeping them in touch with each other's achievements."

At first, *The Sportswoman* devoted an awful lot of its pages to field hockey. But an ad in that premier issue promised coverage of basketball, soccer, fencing, swimming, baseball, water polo, and several other sports. "Through its columns players will be kept in touch with all school, college, club, and association activities," the ad promised. Articles mainly reported the news—the results of games and tournaments as well as the plans of different sports organizations—or were instructional, sharing tips or strategies or even teaching the rules of unfamiliar sports such as lacrosse. As *The Sportswoman* grew in pages and prestige, it would feature pieces by national champions, including Glenna Collett (golf), Helen Jacobs (tennis), and Maribel Vinson (figure skating). Though modest in appearance, this mostly black-and-white magazine was revolutionary, allowing women to control their own media coverage and share ideas on sports among

Reprinted from the *Chicago Tribune*

AUGUST 26, 1925

Girl Athletes

Helen Wills, the nineteen year old California girl, retained the American tennis championship by defeating the British challenger, Kitty McKane, Monday at Forest Hills, New York, 3–6, 6–0, 6–2. An hour later she returned to the courts and with Mary Browne won the doubles championship from May Sutton Bundy and Elizabeth Ryan, 6–4, 6–3. Two championships in one afternoon's hard play. It was a display of energy, endurance, muscle, and skill.

Miss Wills is the new American type of girl. Gertrude Ederle, another American girl, nearly swam the English channel and may try again. Only five men, we believe, have succeeded in this swim. It means a great battle against cold and tides. There is Glenna Collett in golf. A girls' crew appeared in *The Tribune* rowing races. The girls' basketball teams are increasing every year the snappiness of their play. They are track athletes. They are developing muscularity and endurance along with their football playing brothers.

This is a decided change in a girl's training from what it was twenty or even ten years ago, reflected in her stride, her manner, and stamina. It ought to be reflected in the future in the generations of American children whose mothers know the value of physical training from having had it and who are educated in the physical care of the body. ★

themselves. It must be noted, however, that *The Sportswoman* focused almost exclusively on upper- and middle-class white women. The magazine did not cover sports played at historically black colleges or working class recreational leagues.

While *The Sportswoman* set its own path as a magazine devoted to women's sports, mainstream newspapers were recognizing the value of assigning female reporters to cover female athletes. In February 1924, the New York *Herald Tribune* hired a recent college graduate named Margaret Goss to write a weekly column titled "Women in Sport." Over the course of 20 months, Margaret, whose sister was tennis champion Eleanor Goss, developed from a cub reporter to a clever commentator. She named her own New York City all-star girls' college basketball team, assessed the efforts put forth by figure skaters, and slyly threw shade on the fairway shots of a golfer, noting, "She never missed a tree or bunker, and was in every bit of water on the course." Goss vividly described the action at the sporting events she attended and gave personality to the athletes she interviewed. Writing about Gertrude Ederle as she prepared for her first attempt to swim across the English Channel in 1925,

CRITIC

BARON PIERRE DE COUBERTIN

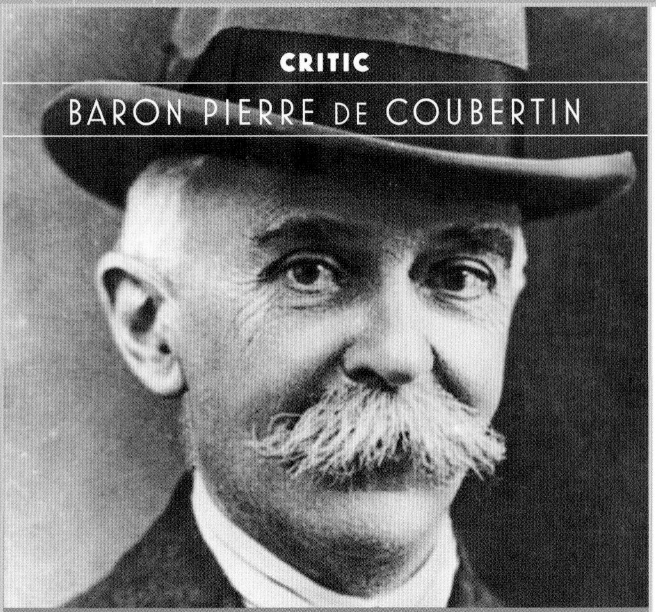

As women gained recognition for their athletic achievements, one powerful critic repeatedly blocked their efforts to participate more fully at the Olympics. Baron Pierre de Coubertin had almost single-handedly revived the Olympic Games in 1896, and he reigned as president of the International Olympic Committee until 1925. From the start, the Frenchman was very clear on what he considered to be the place of women at his sports festival. "Women have but one task, that of the role of crowning the winner with garlands," he said. "In public competitions, women's participation must be absolutely prohibited."

Coubertin's views were shaped in the 19th century. He was born into an aristocratic Parisian family in 1863 and was educated at a Jesuit boarding school. Despite his small stature, he excelled at boxing, rowing, fencing, and horseback riding. Coubertin considered sports an excellent way to build moral character in men and developed the modern Olympic Games to promote athleticism and international goodwill. Although he tried mightily to limit the participation of female athletes, he could not stop the world around him from changing. Since the 1890s, women had started riding bicycles, driving cars, working outside the home, and—in many countries—voting. And thanks to the efforts of Alice Milliat and others, they slowly won the right to do more than just crown the male winners at the Olympics. Pierre de Coubertin died on September 2, 1937, at age 74.

"The average girl who goes into sports will soon cease to be an average girl and become a super one."

—"Minerva's Mail," *Lincoln* (Nebraska) *Star*, September 27, 1925

Goss described a young woman "who loves to swim the same way that other people love to eat candy."

Thanks in part to Goss and the Apple, coverage of women's sports in 1924 and 1925 had more depth and character than ever before. And despite the best efforts of Lou Henry Hoover, female athletes were starting to stand out as they competed in more high-profile events. One such event was the first ever Winter Olympics in Chamonix, France. Figure skating and then ice hockey had been medal sports at previous Olympics, but the IOC decided there was enough interest to hold an International Winter Sports Week—later renamed the First Winter Olympic Games—from

Individual women's figure skating medalists (left to right) Herma Planck-Szabo of Hungary (gold), Ethel Muckelt of Great Britain (bronze), and Beatrix Loughran of the U.S. (silver) celebrate their victories at the 1924 Winter Olympics.

Gertrude Ederle (left) and the rest of the powerful U.S. swimming and diving team pose at the edge of the pool at the 1924 Summer Olympics in Paris, France.

January 25 to February 5, 1924. Sixteen nations sent a total of 247 men and 11 women to compete in 16 events. Women only took part in individual and pairs figure skating, but one of the two Americans, New Yorker Beatrix Loughran, came away with the individual silver medal. Loughran would return to the Winter Games in 1928 to win the individual bronze and in 1932 to take the pairs silver (with Sherwin Badger).

Female athletes had more of a presence at the 1924 Summer Olympics than they'd had at the 1920 Games, but there were still no women's track-and-field events despite the campaign by Alice Milliat. The United States sent 24 women (and 275 men) to those Paris games to vie for medals in swimming, diving, fencing, and tennis. All of the women were white, but a black man, DeHart Hubbard, would win a gold medal in the running long jump for the U.S. Once again,

Helen Wills (left) reaches for a shot as her doubles partner, Hazel Hotchkiss Wightman, looks on during a match at the 1924 Summer Olympics. Wills and Wightman won the gold medal.

American women dominated the diving and swimming competitions, taking 5 of the 6 diving medals and 10 of the 15 swimming medals. Aileen Riggin became the first woman to medal in two different sports at the same Olympics when she won silver in the 3-meter springboard diving contest and bronze in the 100-meter backstroke. Eighteen-year-old Gertrude Ederle made her first splash on the international swimming scene by winning three medals: a gold in the 4 x 100-meter freestyle relay and bronze medals in the 100-meter and 400-meter freestyle races. But perhaps the most celebrated American woman at the 1924 Summer Games was tennis player Helen Wills. "This American schoolgirl has won her championships without losing her poise," reported the *Chicago Tribune*. "That is an achievement." The 18-year-old earned gold medals in singles and doubles (with Hazel Wightman). On the way back home to California, she stopped in New York City to win the singles, doubles (with Wightman again), and mixed doubles (with Vincent Richards) at the U.S. Nationals tournament (now the U.S. Open).

Reprinted from the
Pittsburgh* (Pennsylvania) *Post-Gazette

NOVEMBER 8, 1925

Actress Is Heralded Films' Girl Athlete

Professional boxers train for a match. Constance Talmadge trains for every picture. The star, who is known as one of the most athletic girls in Hollywood, achieves vivacity by keeping physically fit. An accomplished equestrienne, swimmer, golfer, tennis player, fencer and boxer, she has added javelin throwing to her training schedule.

In her next starring vehicle, "East of the Setting Sun," Miss Talmadge will have a role that calls for unusual agility. She must repulse the unwelcome attentions of a gentlemanly villain, as played by Erich von Stroheim, and an unerring aim with impromptu weapons required intensive practice.

When Howard Chandler Christy recently painted a portrait of Miss Talmadge attired in a riding habit, she was described by some as the "typical American girl." She prides herself on always being in condition. Between pictures she spends considerable time in a gymnasium suit or sport clothes. ★

America in 1924 was quite taken with Helen Wills. An estimated crowd of 10,000 turned out to see her beat Molla Mallory in the U.S. Nationals singles final, and her victory was proclaimed in banner headlines. The *Chicago Tribune* declared, "Miss Wills has had more headlines than Mary Pickford," referring to the movie star whose marriage to heartthrob Douglas Fairbanks had set the nation aflutter in 1920. But after her whirlwind summer, Wills returned to study art at the University of California, Berkeley, where she was a sophomore. "Little Miss Poker Face," as she was called because of her steely demeanor on the court, planned to take the rest of the year off from tennis, save one state tournament. Even so, she continued to make news. When sportswriter Grantland Rice put together his list of "ten individuals who have turned in the most noteworthy, commendable and brilliant performance(s) of the year in all sport," Wills was the only woman.

On the American Tennis Association circuit, a new champion was emerging. Ora Washington of Philadelphia took up tennis in 1924 as a way to heal after the death of her sister. Almost immediately she earned high praise as well as a string of victories. "Miss Washington is one of the best net players among women and smashes with the speed and precision of the best male players," reported the Camden, New Jersey, *Courier-Post*, a

TRAILBLAZER

— HELEN FILKEY —

As Helen Wills was racking up tennis titles from Paris to California, another Helen was stockpiling track-and-field records. Before she turned 16 in 1924, Helen Filkey had set a world record in the running broad jump and a U.S. record in the 100-yard dash. But that was just the beginning. By the end of 1925, the Chicago native held world records in the running broad jump (17 feet), the 100-yard dash (11.4 seconds), and the 60-yard hurdles (8.3 seconds), and had earned praise as "the best athlete in the world."

More than a few male reporters criticized female track stars for being ungraceful or even manly, but the press only had praise for Filkey. "She runs like a fawn, and is fairly sylph-like when she leaps a hurdle," wrote Lincoln Quarberg of the *United Press*. "She doesn't scowl or grimace while breaking world's athletic records. She just smiles, while her dark eyes twinkle merrily."

Although some women's track-and-field events were added to the Olympics in 1928, Filkey never got to compete. Neither the hurdles nor the broad jump were on the Olympic program, and she fell in the trials for the 100-meter sprint. (Fellow Chicagoan Betty Robinson won the gold in that event.) Hoping to make the team in 1932, Filkey ran up against the powerful AAU president Avery Brundage. Brundage determined that Filkey's job at a company that sold athletic trophies made her a professional who could profit from her athletic success. Because the Olympics at the time were open only to amateurs, he ruled that she was ineligible. Helen Filkey DeVry, who set 26 world records during her career, died November 24, 2000, at age 92.

Helen Filkey didn't have running clothes when she first started competing, so she wore her brother's bathing trunks.

ATA champion Ora Washington shows off some of her tennis awards in the late 1930s. By the end of her career, she would amass a total of 201 trophies in tennis and basketball.

mainstream newspaper, in 1925. That year she beat singles champion Izzy Channels in the first round of a New York State tournament, but Washington's best days were yet to come. She would win the ATA singles championship every year from 1929 through 1935, and then again in 1937. Also in 1925, she won the ATA national doubles championship with partner Lulu Ballard. It was the first of her 12 consecutive national doubles titles. In the 1930s, Washington would follow in Channels's footsteps as a standout basketball star, leading the team sponsored by the *Philadelphia Tribune,* a black newspaper.

In 1925, another black paper, the *Pittsburgh Courier,* decided to launch a basketball league for black girls and young women. "The so-called 'weaker' sex have made wonderful progress in picking up the rudiments and some of the finer points of the game," the newspaper declared on September 19. The *Courier* pointed to the previous year's Western Pennsylvania championship game, which attracted 500 dedicated fans, as an example of the potential of girls' basketball. Organizers started small with only four teams, but they also invited out-of-town clubs to challenge them. They played under boys' rules, which allowed for more aggressive competition than the girls' rules used in many women's games.

On December 17, the team from Wheeling, West Virginia, defeated the squad from Canonsburg, Pennsylvania, 13 to 9, in the league's first contest.

While the ***Pittsburgh Courier*** not only celebrated female athletes, but also organized opportunities for them to compete, many reporters in the mainstream press still couldn't come to terms with women excelling at sports. According to historian Susan K. Cahn, these sportswriters tried "to reconcile the 'masculine' nature of women's accomplishments with the femininity the public (and they themselves) wanted to see." Toward that end, they emphasized details in the appearance or personal lives of athletes that showed they were just "regular" girls at heart. A profile of Pennsylvania basketball star Dora Lurie was typical, making sure readers knew that besides being unrivaled on the court, "Dora can sew—and knit—and cook." And in 1924, a syndicated article about Helen Wills went so far as to include a special sidebar citing her virtuous qualities. Titled "The Paragon!," the sidebar listed, "No bobbed hair. No cigarettes. No beaded eyelashes. No boisterousness. No 'freshness.' No jazz. BUT—Modesty. Dignity. Simplicity. Athletics. Wholesomeness. 'Good fellow.'"

Even though they couldn't quite figure out female athletes, most male sports reporters at least paid lip service to their talents. But columnist Paul Gallico was the exception. When he looked back at the 1920s in his book *Farewell to Sport,* he expressed utter contempt for athletic women. "No matter how good they are they can never be good enough, quite, to matter," wrote Gallico, who also served as sports editor of the New York *Daily News*. Gallico claimed that newspapers covered women's events only so they could show pictures of scantily clad athletes. He also lambasted females in track and field, writing, "If there is anything more dreadful aesthetically or more depressing than the fatigue-distorted face of a girl runner at the finish line, I have never seen it." Fortunately, female athletes did not need his approval. In fact, on a number of fronts, 1926 was poised to be a breakout year for women in sports.

Helen Filkey shows that despite outperforming most other women in track competitions, she can still bake a cake.

ALSO IN 1924–25

Female athletes were gaining increased recognition and acceptance in 1924 and 1925, but the nation as a whole was grappling with questions of American identity. What did it mean to be an American, and who should be able to claim that title? These questions inspired artists and writers to produce important, insightful work, but they drove others to reject outsiders and discriminate against people who were different from themselves. This led to policies that would impact the course of American history. Here are some noteworthy developments from 1924 and 1925.

1924

✷ J. EDGAR HOOVER

MAY 10, 1924: President Calvin Coolidge appoints J. Edgar Hoover director of the Bureau of Investigation (later called the Federal Bureau of Investigation, or FBI). Hoover, who had carried out raids to catch suspected radicals after World War I, is tasked with cleaning up the image of the federal government in light of the Teapot Dome scandal. He starts by rewriting the qualifications for federal agents, requiring that they have college educations and that they be male. Hoover would run the FBI until his death in 1972. Although he would create a modern, scientific, crime-fighting organization, he also would be accused of abusing his power by compiling secret files on politicians and civil rights leaders and using them to his advantage.

J. Edgar Hoover at his desk, December 1924

✷ IMMIGRATION QUOTAS

MAY 26, 1924: The Immigration Act of 1924 goes into effect, banning immigration from East Asia entirely and introducing a strict quota system to drastically limit the number of Italians, Slavs, Jews, and others from southern and eastern Europe. Proponents of the act seek to preserve an American identity based on the country's earliest white population, many of whom were of northern and western European decent. These advocates claim the people targeted for quotas are too weak and needy to contribute to America's economy, and accuse Asians of not trying to fit into American society. They also fear that radicals from Europe will spread communism, a system that favors giving everyone an equal share of a nation's resources rather than encouraging private ownership and individual profits. The Immigration Act would be revised in 1952 and replaced in 1965.

Immigrant children entering the United States at Ellis Island, in New York Harbor, December 1918

✷ THE LOST GENERATION

APRIL 10, 1925: F. Scott Fitzgerald's novel *The Great Gatsby* is published, introducing the world to millionaire bootlegger Jay Gatsby and his obsession with the beautiful Daisy Buchanan. Fitzgerald is one of a new generation of writers who remember the ravages of World War I and find it hard to enjoy the extravagant, uninhibited America of the 1920s. Their work reveals a sense of emptiness as they struggle to find meaning in a world where everyone seems to be making money and having fun. This "lost generation" of writers includes women as well as men. Gertrude Stein, Dorothy Parker, and poet Edna St. Vincent Millay help shape the literature of the day alongside Fitzgerald, Sinclair Lewis, Ernest Hemingway, and Theodore Dreiser.

F. Scott Fitzgerald

✷ SCOPES MONKEY TRIAL

JULY 10–21, 1925: Science goes head-to-head with the Bible in *The State of Tennessee v. John Thomas Scopes*, often called the Scopes Monkey Trial. In March, the Tennessee legislature had made it illegal for schools to cover the theory of human evolution because it contradicted the teachings of the Bible. The ACLU hoped to test that law with the case of Scopes, who admitted to teaching evolution. With famed attorneys Clarence Darrow for the defense and William Jennings Bryan for the prosecution, the trial generates massive press coverage. In the end, Scopes is found guilty and fined $100. Tennessee's law would not be repealed until 1967. A year later, the U.S. Supreme Court would declare that teaching about evolution could not be prohibited in any U.S. public school.

Scopes trial attorneys Clarence Darrow (left) and William Jennings Bryan

1925

✷ ART DECO

APRIL TO OCTOBER, 1925: An exhibition of decorative and industrial arts in Paris, France, gives a name to the modern, geometric style of art and design that had been evolving since just before World War I: art deco. With its symmetry and hard lines, art deco often combines metals with other materials to emphasize technological progress with a nod to the future. It finds expression in the design of everything from buildings and trains to household products such as lamps and radios. (This book is designed in the art deco style.) New York City's Chrysler Building is an iconic example of art deco architecture. The heyday of art deco design would end with the rise of a less luxurious modern style during World War II.

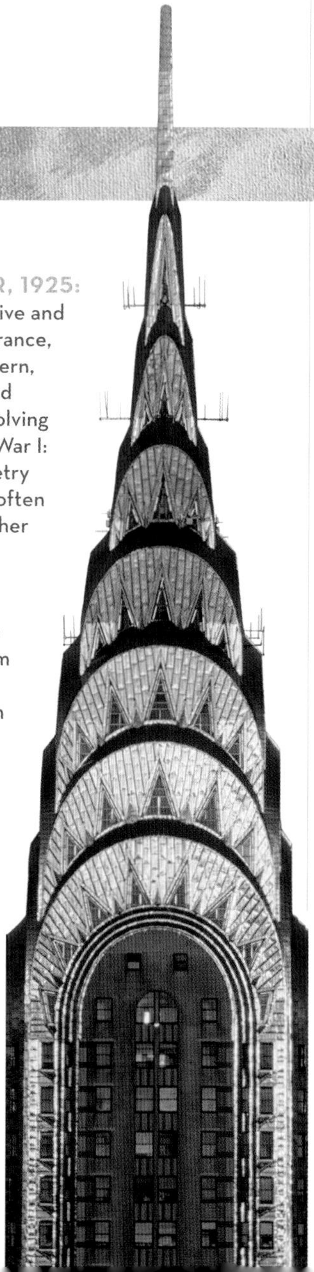

The Chrysler Building in New York City, completed in 1930

Ku Klux Klan members march in Washington, D.C., with the Capitol in the background.

✷ THE KLAN RALLIES

AUGUST 8, 1925: Some 40,000 members of the Ku Klux Klan in white robes and pointed hoods march down Pennsylvania Avenue in Washington, D.C., in a defiant rally to assert their right to assemble. The Klan, infamous for promoting white supremacy and racism through intimidation and violence in the South immediately after the Civil War, experienced a rebirth after World War I. As black Americans migrated north in search of economic opportunities and northern cities saw an influx of immigrants, the Klan played on people's prejudices. It positioned itself as a fraternal organization for white Protestants and promoted "One Hundred Percent Americanism." But soon after the Washington rally, one powerful leader would be convicted of rape and murder, destroying the myth of the Klan as a law-abiding organization and leading to a rapid decline in its membership.

"[It was] a simple game of tennis, yet a game which made continents stand still, and was the most important sporting event of modern times exclusively in the hands of the fair sex."

—Ferdinand Tuohy, *New York Times*, February 17, 1926

Suzanne Lenglen (left) and Helen Wills arrive on court for their history-making match. Always fashionable, Lenglen wears her signature turban and mink-trimmed coat.

CHAPTER 4

CELEBRATING VICTORIES

— 1926–27 —

Helen Wills nearly boycotted the most important tennis match of her career. The match—referred to as the "Battle of the Century" by reporters—pitted the California college student against the veteran Suzanne Lenglen of France, considered by many to be the best female player in the world. The two had never gone head-to-head, but they were on track to meet in the finals of a 1926 tournament near Lenglen's home on the French Riviera. Sensing the opportunity of a lifetime, tennis fans flocked to France, snatching up tickets that originally sold for 50 francs ($12.50) but were inflated to five times that much. Newspaper and radio reporters did, too, mesmerized by the thought of a meeting between the virtuous Wills and the fiery Lenglen. When Wills heard that American newsreel camera operators would not be allowed to film the contest, however, she threatened not to take part.

"The glory of achievement in almost every sport for girls is written in glowing colors for all the world to see. The public who once scorned, now pays homage to the girl athletes."

—Jane Grey, *Oakland* (California) *Tribune*, December 5, 1926

Wills was incensed that an American millionaire had bought the movie rights to the match for $100,000. "It seems to me a shame that a game of amateur tennis ... should be distorted into a money-making scheme to enrich commercial speculators," Wills told reporters. After Lenglen joined Wills in her protest, the millionaire released the rights, inviting the newsreel operators to film for free. The incident only served to intensify interest in the match. "Never has the Riviera been like this before," sportswriter John Tunis observed. "People who until last week did not know whether tennis was a game or something to eat now discuss footwork and a difference in balls or climate with the greatest authority." By the time the

Spectators fill the stadium and even perch precipitously on rooftops as they watch Wills, foreground, serve to Lenglen in the match that was labeled the "Battle of the Century."

two women played on February 16, 1926, their audience had swelled to 5,000.

Although the gallery was overwhelmingly rooting for "Sizzling Suzanne," the speedy local champion showed her nerves. "Suzanne's game was built on control of the ball and placing it to open the court," journalist Allison Danzig later remembered. "The day she played Helen she was nervous and she missed shots she never did ordinarily." Lenglen found her opponent's powerful ground strokes and competitive spirit so unsettling that she drank brandy during the changeovers to calm herself. In the end, Lenglen rallied to win, 6–3, 8–6. Fans and reporters immediately started talking about a rematch, but Lenglen soon turned professional, so she could no longer compete against Wills, who remained an amateur. Though they would never play each other again, their meeting stood as a pivotal moment in women's sports. It was the first time that a contest with female competitors inspired the intense fervor associated with the most thrilling men's sporting events.

Just six months later, another member of the "fair sex" would record an athletic achievement that arguably surpassed the Battle of the Century in both significance and drama. Once again it happened in Europe, but the protagonist was a New Yorker: 20-year-old Olympic gold medalist Gertrude Ederle. On June 10, 1926, Ederle arrived at Cap Gris-Nez, France, to

Reprinted from the *Columbus* (Nebraska) *Telegram*

JANUARY 13, 1927

Make Training Rules for Women Athletes

University Girls Will Follow Same Routine as Men

LINCOLN, JAN. 13 (U.P.)—Equal rights for women have been provided by the women's athletic association of the University of Nebraska in establishing training rules pertaining to women athletes.

Hereafter women athletes at the university must observe the following training rules, which are similar to those of men athletes:

- Eight hours sleep.
- Three "regular" meals a day.
- Fresh fruit, milk and water between meals, but no delicacies.
- A 30 minute brisk walk daily.

Five violations of the training rules expel the women athletes from future seasonal athletic competition. The only exception to the eight-hour sleep rule is during examination periods when the rules committee admitted that many hours of night "cramming" are sometimes necessary. ★

CRITIC

BLANCHE M. TRILLING

Like Lou Henry Hoover, Blanche M. Trilling was an advocate for women and believed that competitive sports were rife with problems. The longtime director of physical education for women at the University of Wisconsin, Trilling was also, with Hoover, one of the founders of the Women's Division of the National Amateur Athletic Federation. In February 1927, Trilling gave a speech enumerating her concerns about the state of "girls' athletics." First she read a lengthy letter from a teacher describing her basketball team's horrific experience at an away game. After recalling the "howling, yelling, yapping, uncouth, and for the most part disrespectful audience," the teacher concluded, "It was all a gladiatorial combat, witnessed by a primitive people yelling they knew not what for."

Trilling said basketball was the main problem in girls' athletics because it was the sport "which all girls want to play." But she also criticized track and field because of its abbreviated uniforms and swimming because athletes were encouraged to set records without regard to the effects on their health. She pointed out that some of the same problems existed in men's sports, but women could correct their course and embrace a more positive approach before the situation got out of hand. She reminded her audience of the value of play days, the events endorsed by the Women's Division, where "competition is wholesome and joyous since every member of the school takes part." Blanche Trilling died on October 10, 1964, at age 88.

prepare for her second attempt to swim across the English Channel. For swimmers, the Channel crossing was the white whale—the goal they relentlessly pursued but often failed to achieve. "The Channel swim satisfies man's elemental urge to pit his puny strength against the cosmic forces of nature," explained journalist George Trevor of the New York *Sun*. The journey, about 21 miles long as the crow flies, was often much longer because shifting tides pushed and pulled swimmers in different directions. Ederle's trainer, Bill Burgess, had failed to make it across a dozen times before finally succeeding in 1911. Besides Burgess, only four men had completed the swim. If Ederle triumphed, she would be the first woman.

Although the summer had been unusually cold and dreary, the sun was shining when Ederle plunged into the surf at 7:09 a.m. on August 6. Soon the only things visible were her red swimming cap, her churning arms, and her goggle-covered face when she came up for air. A tugboat followed close behind, carrying Ederle's father, sister, trainer, and well-wishers, as well as a few journalists, photographers, and a wireless operator to document the journey. The wireless operator would turn the journalists' reports into Morse code and send them by radio waves to newspapers in the United States. Ederle's father, who served as her manager, had made an exclusive deal with the *Chicago Tribune* newspaper syndicate, owners of the New York *Daily News*. Ederle would write columns about her swim for the syndicate, and only its photographers and reporters, including a surprisingly enthusiastic Paul Gallico, would have the inside track on her story. Others would be left to report on the swim without doing one-on-one interviews or enjoying a spot on the family's tugboat. In exchange for their exclusive, the *Tribune* syndicate would pay Ederle $5,000 and cover her training expenses. She would earn a $2,500 bonus if she swam all the way to England.

Conditions were perfect during the first five hours of Ederle's swim, but around noon the wind picked up, getting stronger with every passing hour.

Gertrude Ederle is covered with four coats of oil and grease to keep her warm and protect her skin from chafing as she begins her second attempt to conquer the English Channel.

Ederle's two-piece swimsuit, made of black silk, is light enough not to weigh her down. Less than a decade earlier, female swimmers were expected to wear swimsuits with skirts as well as heavy woolen leggings.

The gusts whipped up the water, and soon Ederle was battling choppy waves and maneuvering around chunks of driftwood and poisonous jellyfish. At about 6 p.m., with rain falling and mighty tides pushing her off course, Ederle's trainer called to her to give up, fearing that she would get hurt. She stopped long enough to yell, "What for?" and kept swimming. When she finally walked unsteadily onto the English shore just north of Kingsdown at 9:48 p.m., the waiting crowd cheered wildly. The trip had taken Ederle 14 hours 39 minutes, which was almost two hours faster than the existing record. The next day, newspapers around the world proclaimed Ederle's victory. Some papers had the presence of mind to ask feminists what they thought about Ederle's feat. "The beauty of these spectacular achievements by any one woman is that they kill off a lot of bugaboos that hinder the rest of women," said Gertrude Foster Brown, managing director of *The Woman Citizen,* a political magazine. "People still say silly things about women being weaklings ... it takes a good drama like this to teach people a lesson!"

TRAILBLAZER

SYBIL BAUER

Gertrude Ederle was not the first woman to beat a men's swimming record. Sybil Bauer did that in 1922. At the time, U.S. Olympian Harold "Stubby" Kruger held the world record in the 440-yard backstroke at 6 minutes 28 seconds. But on a trip to Bermuda, Bauer, still a teenager, beat it by 3.2 seconds. In February 1924, she bettered that time, swimming the distance in 6 minutes 23 seconds. Bauer was an acclaimed backstroker. In her lifetime, she set 23 world records and at one point held the world records for every women's backstroke distance. At the 1924 Summer Olympics in Paris, she won the gold medal in the only women's backstroke distance contested: 100 meters.

Bauer was born in Chicago in 1903 and started swimming in high school at age 15. After high school, she entered Northwestern University, serving as president of the Woman's Athletic Association and playing varsity field hockey when she wasn't swimming. In 1926, after winning her sixth consecutive national Amateur Athletic Union title in the 100-yard backstroke, she became ill. Her family kept the severity of her illness from the public, so people were shocked on January 31, 1927, to hear that she had died. She was only 23 years old and had recently become engaged to sportswriter Edward Sullivan, who decades later would host his own groundbreaking TV variety show.

Although the cause of Bauer's death was cancer, the secrecy surrounding her illness allowed some critics of women's sports to spread misinformation for their own purposes. "The early death of this brilliant young woman is a warning against too violent exercise," wrote journalist Arthur Brisbane. "Straining the heart means shortening life."

Sybil Bauer held eight national and world records in the backstroke at the time of her death.

One incentive during Gertrude Ederle's English Channel swim was the promise of a new red Buick roadster if she made it across. The *Daily News* gave her the car.

Gertrude Ederle was one of more than a dozen men and women who attempted to swim the Channel in 1926. Four others made it that year, including another woman: Danish-born American Amelia "Mille" Gade Corson. On August 27–28, she crossed from France to England in 15 hours 29 minutes, becoming the first mother to complete the swim. But it was Ederle who inspired the imaginations of people from all communities and demographic groups. On February 5, 1927, the *Pittsburgh Courier* announced it would endeavor to create interest in swimming among black women and men across the U.S. by supporting an aspiring marathon swimmer named Ellen Ray. "The *Pittsburgh Courier* has faith in the athletic ability of the colored womanhood of America," the paper explained, "and believe if our women are encouraged and urged forward, they too can establish good records and set high marks." Ray planned to attempt a 17-mile swim in New York's Hudson River as a first step. Unfortunately, in early May, she was seriously injured when the doors of a New York City subway car closed on her, crushing her ribs and causing her to abandon her effort.

"When two American women can successfully swim the English Channel ... it means that women are being developed here with an endurance, strength, courage and skill which may one day make them the equal of men in physical prowess."

—Katherine Lipke, "New Race of Women," *Los Angeles Times*, September 5, 1926

Despite Ellen Ray's misfortune, women were making their mark in sports in 1926, and some men were starting to get uneasy. In November 1926, *Popular Science Monthly*, which had an overwhelmingly male audience, ran a long article titled "Why Men Beat Women at Sports." Author Arthur Grahame started by admitting dismay that both Ederle and Corson had swum the English Channel faster than all previous men. He then expressed relief that both men who made the swim after Corson in 1926 beat Ederle's record time. "Which was as it should be," wrote Grahame, "for despite male fears and feminine achievement, man remains supreme in sports, and, in the opinion of many experts well qualified to judge, will remain supreme in sports for many generations—probably forever." After that pronouncement, Grahame looked at swimming, tennis, golf, and track and field, each time declaring the best female athletes inferior to men in their sports. He concluded, "Men, it seems, are able to beat women in sports just because they are men, endowed by nature with superior qualities of speed, strength, and stamina!"

Grahame's article aimed to reframe women's triumphs as failures. In an effort to protect his sense of the balance of power

Reprinted from the *Pittsburgh* (Pennsylvania) *Courier*

JUNE 18, 1927

Girls, Be Athletic!

While dozens of our girls participated in the meet Thursday, there was a notable absence of such a versatile young girl athlete as Miss Ruth Allen was in her days of participation in scholastic sports. There is a splendid chance for fine physical development, glory for one's school and personal honor through the channel of athletic endeavors; so girls, don't miss the chance to take part in the various sports sanctioned by your schools. ★

Kinue Hitomi (265), shown here in 1928, received an honorary prize from Alice Milliat for the best individual performance at the 1926 Women's World Games.

in society, he created a competition between male and female athletes that didn't really exist. Very few women wanted to go head-to-head with men in sports. Rather, they sought to excel on their own terms, to reach personal bests, and compete against other women. But Grahame found the accomplishments of Gertrude Ederle and other female athletes so threatening that he systematically tore them down, woman by woman, sport by sport, informing his readers that while these athletes were good, they weren't good enough. This strategy set a precedent that would be repeated by male sportswriters whenever women athletes reached new heights for decades to come.

Just a few weeks after Ederle's Channel swim, Alice Milliat held another Women's Games to demonstrate why the IOC should add women's track and field to the next Summer Olympics. Athletes from nine nations traveled to Gothenburg, Sweden, to compete in a dozen events at the 1926 Women's World Games in late August. The star of the track meet was Kinue Hitomi of Japan, who comprised her country's entire team. She won gold medals in the running long jump and the standing long jump, a silver in the discus throw, and a bronze in the 100-yard race. She also came in fifth in the 60-meter sprint and sixth in the 250-meter run. Thanks to the continued pressure from Milliat and the retirement of IOC president Pierre de Coubertin, the IOC finally voted to add five events in women's track and field to the 1928 Summer Games.

Not all the inroads in women's sports in 1926 and 1927 took place on the international level. In spite of the continued efforts of the Women's Division of the NAAF to limit competition, many recreation centers in the U.S. were building strong programs for female athletes. In Minneapolis, Minnesota, for example, women at the Phyllis Wheatley Settlement House could compete in track and field and play basketball and diamond ball, an early form of softball. The neighborhood center, founded to serve the black community (and still in existence today), sponsored a women's diamond ball team in the Intermediate Settlement House League. Diamond ball was quickly becoming popular elsewhere, too, with community leagues in Florida, Wisconsin, Iowa, and South Dakota, among other states. Some schools even fielded diamond ball teams.

In the final years of the Roaring Twenties, however, this forward progress in women's sports would hit a roadblock. Concerned female physical educators and self-righteous male commentators would come together to express alarm about the impact of competition on women's mental and physical health. The debate would blow up during the Summer Olympics on August 2, 1928, in a sport that had already received its fair share of negative press: track and field.

Among the players on the Phyllis Wheatley Intermediate Diamond Ball Team was Ethel Ray Nance (top left), who went on to become the first black policewoman in Minneapolis, Minnesota, secretary to civil rights activist W. E. B. Du Bois, and co-founder of the San Francisco African-American Historical and Cultural Society in California.

ALSO IN 1926–27

Gertrude Ederle, Helen Wills, and Suzanne Lenglen were hardly the only heroes to emerge in 1926 and 1927. It seemed that every day, Americans were reading about individuals who were breaking barriers or otherwise making their mark on the world. They also were reading more in general, thanks to a new way of getting books to people who might live miles from the nearest bookstore. Here are some heroic developments from 1926 and 1927.

1926

✷ BOOKS IN THE MAIL

APRIL 16, 1926: Harry Scherman, a New York advertising copywriter, and his two partners send out close to 5,000 copies of the first selection in their new Book of the Month Club: Sylvia Townsend Warner's feminist novel *Lolly Willowes, Or the Loving Huntsman*. Subscribers in the club sign up for monthly deliveries of books chosen by a distinguished "selecting committee" of authors, educators, critics, and journalists. Scherman predicts that his club will help publishers introduce new books and unknown authors to large audiences. Indeed, by its 25th anniversary, the Book of the Month Club would mail out more than 100 million books.

Sharpshooter Annie Oakley in London, England, 1892

✷ ANNIE OAKLEY DIES

NOVEMBER 3, 1926: Americans mourn the end of an era when sharpshooter Annie Oakley dies at age 66 in her hometown of Greenville, Ohio. Born Phoebe Ann Moses, Oakley was one of the first internationally known female sports stars. From 1885 through 1901, she displayed her target-shooting skills with Buffalo Bill's Wild West, a traveling show that reenacted stories from the American frontier. Oakley performed in Europe as well as in the United States and often accepted target-shooting challenges from men in the places she visited. (She usually won.) "With the disappearance of Annie Oakley," writes one newspaper, "a strong link between the heroic past and the practical present is snapped ... The inspiration of the old frontier is gone."

✷ *HOMESPUN HEROINES*

1926: Hallie Quinn Brown publishes *Homespun Heroines and Other Women of Distinction*, a compilation of biographies and pictures of close to 60 notable black women born in North America in the 18th and 19th centuries. The book presents the stories of famous as well as lesser-known women, including doctors, lawyers, teachers, and more. Brown herself is the daughter of two former slaves. While she was growing up in the 1850s and early 1860s in Pittsburgh, Pennsylvania, her house served as a station on the Underground Railroad, where fugitive slaves could seek refuge. After graduating from the historically black Wilberforce College in Ohio, she became an educator, activist, author, and public speaker.

Hallie Quinn Brown in Xenia, Ohio, circa 1880

✷ THE GREAT BAMBINO

SEPTEMBER 30, 1927: George Herman "Babe" Ruth, Jr., of the New York Yankees sets a single-season home run record when he slugs his 60th in a game against the Washington Senators. Ruth's record would stand for 34 years before being broken by Roger Maris, also of the Yankees, who would hit 61 in 1961. Referred to by reporters as the "Great Bambino" and the "Sultan of Swat," Ruth is a larger-than-life character. During his 22 seasons in the major leagues, he would hit 714 home runs and bat .342. In 1936, a year after retiring, Ruth would be one of the first five players elected to the new National Baseball Hall of Fame in Cooperstown, New York. (The others were Honus Wagner, Christy Mathewson, Walter Johnson, and Ty Cobb.)

Babe Ruth hitting a home run for the New York Yankees

1927

✷ LUCKY LINDY

MAY 21, 1927: Charles A. Lindbergh, a 25-year-old airmail pilot from Detroit, Michigan, becomes the first person to successfully complete a solo transatlantic flight when he flies his *Spirit of St. Louis* from Long Island, New York, to Paris, France, in 33 hours 30 minutes. An estimated 100,000 people greet "Lucky Lindy" when he lands, but that is just a fraction of the millions who would celebrate his heroics during a subsequent U.S. cross-country tour. Lindbergh's flight would be a boon for the aviation industry, with investors creating several commercial carriers in the next few years. Amelia Earhart, who would soon set her own flying records, would sometimes be called "Lady Lindy" because of her physical resemblance to Lindbergh.

In February 1928, Charles Lindbergh poses with his plane, the *Spirit of St. Louis*, in St. Louis, Missouri.

Duke Ellington (with baton) and his band, 1931

✷ THE DUKE OF HARLEM

DECEMBER 4, 1927: Edward Kennedy "Duke" Ellington and his jazz orchestra begin a four-year stint as the house band at the Cotton Club, a nightclub and speakeasy in New York City. Although it is located in Harlem—the center of the explosion in black arts and literature that would become known as the Harlem Renaissance—the Cotton Club accepts only white patrons, who flock there to enjoy entertainment by black artists. Ellington, who earned his nickname because of his dignified manner, would gain national prominence from his Cotton Club gig, releasing record albums, performing on stage and radio, and working in films. Playing piano and composing many of his group's hits, Ellington would prove to be a giant in the history of jazz—the music that set the syncopated beat of the 1920s and beyond.

"Women's athletics today are at the crossroads. Which way they turn will mean much in the future for American sport and for the womanhood of the country."

—John R. Tunis, *Harper's Monthly Magazine*, July 1929

Japan's Kinue Hitomi (left) gives Germany's Lina Radke a run for her money in the contentious 800-meter race at the 1928 Summer Olympics in the Netherlands.

CHAPTER 5

FACING NEW CHALLENGES

— 1928–29 —

Initial reports chronicling the women's 800-meter race at the 1928 Summer Olympics in Amsterdam, the Netherlands, recounted a thrilling contest. "The 800-metre women runners gave the immense crowd the thrill of the afternoon," wrote W. H. Ingram, the Canadian press correspondent. "The women got off to a beautiful start and rounded the first curve at a stiff pace." Ingram described Germany's Lina Radke pulling away from Japan's Kinue Hitomi and the other seven runners as she entered the final straightaway. "Radke opened up and took the lead," Ingram wrote. "The German girl spurted to cross the tape seven seconds under the world's record for the distance." The correspondent for the Associated Press painted a similar picture: "Radke, after traveling a sensational pace for a woman, was barely able to withstand a closing rush by the strong Japanese runner."

"In my opinion, the 1928 Olympics have proven just once more that women have earned a permanent place in sports. The discussion as to whether women's events should be a part of the next Olympics was a pathetic anachronism."

—Ruth Drucille Rickaby, *The Sportswoman*, October 1928

Both reporters noted the race was so fast that each of the first six runners beat the existing women's world record.

Yet that is not how the race is remembered. Other reporters, most notably Wythe Williams of the *New York Times*, changed the narrative by exaggerating the toll the race took on the women. "The final of the women's 800-meter run," he wrote, "plainly demonstrated that even this distance makes too great a call on feminine strength. At the finish, six out of the nine runners were completely exhausted and fell headlong on the ground. Several had to be carried off the track." Williams, who was a foreign correspondent and not a sports

Nine women from six different nations spring forward at the start of the 800-meter race at the 1928 Summer Olympics. Two years earlier, women had run a 1,000-meter race at the Women's World Games.

reporter, failed to understand that it was fairly common for runners to lunge and sometimes fall at the end of a race—or even to collapse in exhaustion. Indeed, two male runners had collapsed at the conclusion of the men's 800 two days earlier, though Williams didn't mention it in his coverage of that event. At any rate, film footage taken at the women's 800 shows the runners striding confidently, with only one, the injured Canadian Jean Thompson, falling at the end. But that didn't stop Williams and other writers from exaggerating accounts of the racers' distress.

These alarmist reports played right into the hands of people who had opposed adding women's track and field to the Olympics. Just five days later, the International Amateur Athletic Federation (IAAF), which governed the sport, met to decide the fate of women's events. Representatives from Canada and a handful of other nations proposed eliminating all women's track-and-field offerings from future Olympic Games. In response, "Frau Dr. Bergman," the physician for the German women's team, reported that decades of tests in her country proved participating in track and field did not physically harm female athletes. What's more, she said competition had not affected Lina Radke's femininity, assuring the group that

CRITIC

POPE PIUS XI

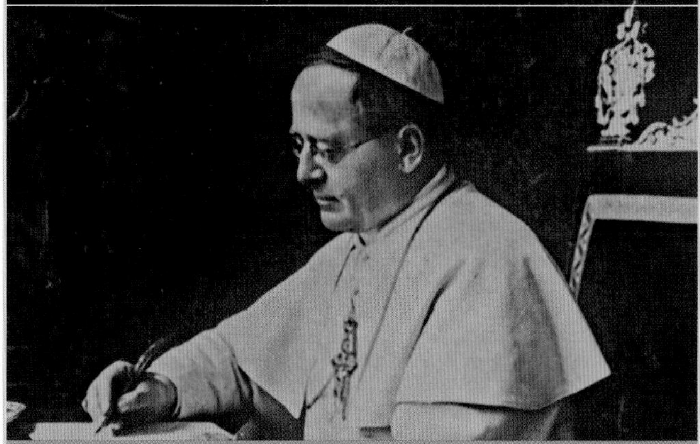

As athletes around the world prepared for the 1928 Summer Olympics, the leader of the Catholic Church condemned the participation of girls and women in public sports events. Pius XI had been elected pope in February 1922. In May 1928, as Italy's Fascist Party prepared to sponsor its first athletic event for girls in Rome, the pope expressed his dismay. He pointed out that ancient Romans excluded females from public athletic competitions and said it was deplorable that in modern times, "sensibility and attention toward the delicate regard due to young women and girls should be weaker than in pagan Rome." The pope said activities that caused women to sacrifice modesty must be avoided, adding, "If a woman's hand must be raised, we hope and pray it may be raised only in prayer or in acts of charity."

Despite the pope's protest, the Fascist Party's competition went on. But Pope Pius continued to speak and write about women's sports, particularly in terms of the clothing athletes wore. In 1930, he issued the church's worldwide policy on women's dress, which included the stipulation that "parents must keep their daughters away from public gymnastic games and competitions unless they are fully and modestly dressed." In subsequent years, however, the pope turned his attention to weightier matters. As the Nazis came to power in Germany, he strongly condemned their white supremacist policies and anti-Semitic actions. He also tried to convince Italy's Fascist government not to accept the racist views of its German allies. Pope Pius XI died on February 10, 1939, at age 81, seven months before the outbreak of World War II.

Reprinted from the *Boston Globe*

JUNE 1, 1929

Eleonora Sears Makes Fast Time

Walks 42 1/2 Miles
in 8 Hours 30 Minutes

PARIS, MAY 31 (A.P.)—After walking 42½ miles in eight hours and 30 minutes, Miss Eleonora Sears of Boston felt "fine" today.

The trained Boston sportswoman and pedestrian started from Fontainebleau at 5:02 a.m. yesterday and arrived at the Ritz Hotel at 1:37 p.m., finishing fresh and chipper. During her hike she took only tea from a thermos bottle provided by friends who accompanied her in an automobile. During the hike she never slackened her pace.

Her time, an average of about five miles an hour, was better than that in previous walks between Newport, R.I., and Boston; Laurel, Md., and Baltimore; and Providence and Boston.

The weather was cool, with no wind, and ideal for walking. ★

Note: Eleonora Sears (1881–1968) was an all-around American athlete who won national tennis and squash titles, raced automobiles and powerboats, flew airplanes, played baseball, hockey, golf, and polo, and rode in equestrian events.

"the world champion cooked, sewed, and kept house like any other *hausfrau*." After a heated debate, delegates rejected the proposal to eliminate all track-and-field events by a vote of 16 to 6. However they did vote 12 to 9 (with one abstention) to remove the 800 from the program for the next Summer Games. The women's 800 would not return to the Olympics until 1960.

Meanwhile, the Women's Division of the NAAF called for the elimination of ALL women's events in ALL sports from the 1932 Summer Games, which were to be held in Los Angeles, California. In their place, the group suggested a separate women's sports festival that would emphasize participation rather than competition. "I would not like to have my sister or any other girl in whom I am interested take part in any proceeding such as the last Olympics," said Ethel Perrin, chair of the Women's Division's Executive Committee. The group's proposal was rejected; female athletes would participate as scheduled at the 1932 Games. But the fight galvanized the Women's Division's efforts to combat competition in school sports. Its annual meeting in January 1929 was a rallying cry for local affiliates "to do all in their power to more actively spread the principles advocated by this Division." That meant developing programs "with the emphasis put upon participation rather than on winning."

Students compete in the low hurdles at the Radcliffe College field day in 1928. An alternative to play days, intramural field days were popular at women's schools and often focused on track-and-field events.

Following the annual meeting, the Women's Division started to get such a steady stream of progress reports from communities across the country that it created a monthly newsletter to share them. Without meaning to, the newsletter documented the deliberate dismantling of women's competitive sports in the nation's high schools and colleges. "The Central Board ... voted to discontinue basketball tournaments held for high school girls," wrote a correspondent from Alabama. "Rochester plays no interschool games for girls in Junior and Senior High Schools," reported a writer from New York. "Houston and Austin are not going to enter teams in the Women's State Basketball Tournament this year and will try to stop plans for one," promised a letter from Texas. As interscholastic leagues disappeared, play days replaced them, to the joy of the Women's Division and the exasperation of competitive athletes throughout the nation.

Still, some schools swam—or ran—against the tide, particularly those in the black community. In February 1929, Tuskegee Institute, a historically black college in Tuskegee, Alabama, announced that female students had voted to form a women's track team: the Tigerettes. Two years earlier, the school had held its

"In view of the services of our women in the World War and to the American Legion and the nation ... it is held that Margaret Gisolo should not be barred [from playing baseball] on account of her sex."

—Dan Sowers, National Director, American Legion Baseball, in the *Arizona Republic* (Phoenix, Arizona), July 22, 1928

first Tuskegee Relays track meet. The meet was designed to offer competition for black male athletes, who at that time were barred from track contests run by the Amateur Athletic Union. Tuskegee invited students from other schools in its Southern Intercollegiate Athletic Conference (SIAC), made up of historically black colleges, to compete at the relays. In 1929, the Tuskegee Relays featured its first two events for women: a 1/4-mile relay and a 100-yard dash.

Cleve Abbott, Tuskegee's director of physical education, hoped to use the relays to develop talented black female athletes who could succeed at the Olympic Games. Black men had been competing at the Olympics since 1900, and runner John Baxter Taylor, Jr., became the first black athlete to win a gold medal in 1908, as part of the U.S. medley relay team. But no black woman had yet to make the U.S. Olympic team. So Abbott kept adding women's events to the Tuskegee Relays: the women's 50-yard dash and discus throw in 1930 and others after that. His strategy would succeed. In 1948, Alice Coachman, a Tuskegee graduate, would win the

After playing American Legion baseball, Margaret Gisolo studied dance and co-founded the School of Dance at Arizona State University. She also became a nationally ranked seniors tennis champion, retiring at age 86.

TRAILBLAZER

— INEZ PATTERSON —

When Inez "Pat" Patterson was an athlete at Temple University in Philadelphia, Pennsylvania, she fought her own quiet battle against racism. A member of the swim team, she was assigned to practice at a specific hour set aside for black women. "I always refused," she told a reporter. "I got around that by always being 'too busy' to do any practicing at that time." Officials had no choice but to let her practice with the rest of the team. Patterson was used to navigating uncomfortable situations. At West Philadelphia High School, from 1925 through 1928, she was the only black student on her field hockey team. She was also a distance swimmer, a basketball player, and a track star, specializing in the shot put.

Patterson studied physical education at Temple, where she made the all-collegiate teams in hockey, basketball, tennis, track, volleyball, and acrobatic dancing. During that time, she also was the swimming director at the Catherine Street Colored YWCA and organized and played on the Y's Quick Steppers girls' basketball team. The team amassed an 11-1 record in 1929-30, and laid claim to the Eastern Colored Women's Basketball Championship. In 1931, Patterson was hired to play for and help coach the *Philadelphia Tribune*'s Newsgirls basketball team. That paper called her the "foremost girl athlete in the city."

After college, Patterson became a physical education teacher and leader with the YWCA, working at various locations in New Jersey and New York. She also served as national program director for the American Tennis Association. Inez Patterson died in 1944. She was in her early 30s.

A 1932 ad in the *Philadelphia Tribune* called Newsgirls Inez Patterson and Ora Washington "two of the greatest girl players in the world" and noted, "They make you forget the Depression."

Olympic gold medal in the high jump. She would be the first black female Olympic gold medalist and the only American woman to win gold at the 1948 Summer Games.

Alice Coachman won 10 AAU high jump championships in a row, from 1939 through 1948. She was unable to compete at the Olympics until 1948, as the 1940 and 1944 Games were canceled because of World War II.

Girls and women also continued to forge new ground outside of school. In 1928, Margaret Gisolo was a shy 13-year-old in Blanford, Indiana, whose big brother, Tony, asked her to play for the American Legion junior baseball team he was coaching. It turned out she was the only girl in a league with 180,000 boys, but no one seemed to mind—until Gisolo drove in the winning run in the 12th inning of a playoff game. Then the opposing team protested, claiming, "The rules had been drawn up to cover a boy's game" and "the game seemed too rough and dangerous for a girl." League officials checked the rule book and didn't find any mention that players had to be boys, so Gisolo and her team continued on through the playoffs. They won the state championship and headed to the regional tournament in Chicago. Although they lost there, Gisolo had earned celebrity status, tagged the "Girl Babe Ruth of Blanford" by the press. But she was to be the last female in the league for decades. In 1929, officials banned girls from playing American Legion baseball. They would not reverse that ruling until the 1970s.

While Gisolo played her championship season, women were reaching new heights in aviation. On June 17–18, 1928, 30-year-old Amelia Earhart became the first woman to fly across the Atlantic Ocean, although she did so as a passenger rather than a pilot. But that was just the beginning of a long list of firsts Earhart would achieve before her disappearance on a round-the-world flight in 1937. In September 1928, she became the first woman to fly solo across the United States and back (with necessary refueling stops along the way). The following year she was one of the participants in the first Women's Air Derby, dubbed the "Powder Puff Derby" by humorist Will Rogers. Earhart finished third in the race, which required the pilots to fly from Santa Monica, California, to Cleveland, Ohio. Also in 1929, she helped found the Ninety-Nines, an international group that aimed "to promote good fellowship among licensed women pilots, encourage flying among women and create opportunities for women in commercial aviation." The group got its name from the number of pilots who came to its first meeting or initially expressed interest in joining.

As the 1920s drew to a close, other women whose names would dominate the sports landscape were just starting to stake out a place for themselves. Norway's Sonja Henie won her first gold medal in figure skating at the 1928 Winter Games. She would repeat at the next two

Daily News

Reprinted from the *Daily News* (New York, New York)

NOVEMBER 23, 1929

Amelia Earhart Breaks Women's Speed Record

LOS ANGELES, NOV. 22 (U.P.)—Amelia Earhart, trans-Atlantic flier, broke the world's speed record for women today, attaining an average unofficial speed of 184.7 miles an hour. Her fastest speed was 197.8 miles. She flew a Lockheed-Vega. Her instruments must be checked at Washington against the 156-miles record held by Mrs. Louise Thaden. Miss Earhart flew a course which totaled four miles, making two one-mile trips with the wind and two against the wind. She carried 150 gallons of gasoline and 12 gallons of oil. ★

Note: Earhart's top speed would be officially confirmed at 197 miles per hour (mph), though her average speed for the four-mile flight would be revised to 158.7 mph. Above, Earhart is shown with an Avron Avian biplane she bought in 1928.

Winter Olympics, win 10 consecutive world champion titles, and then move to Hollywood to star in a series of successful films. In 1929, Ora Washington won the first of her string of eight national American Tennis Association singles titles. A few years later, she would start to dominate on the basketball court for the *Philadelphia Tribune* Newsgirls team. She would barnstorm with the team for a dozen years, playing against both black and white squads all over the South, Midwest, and East. When she wasn't playing sports, she was earning a living as a housekeeper. And in Texas, a scout from the Employers Casualty Insurance Company was just about to offer Mildred "Babe" Didrikson a job so she could play on their basketball team. At the same time, she was honing her skills in track and field, which she would use to win two gold medals and one silver at the 1932 Summer Olympics. Didrikson would later become a champion golfer and be named the Greatest Female Athlete of the First Half of the [Twentieth] Century by the Associated Press.

With three consecutive gold medals, Sonja Henie remains the most decorated ladies singles figure skater in the history of the Olympic Games.

Still, the triumphs of these stars did not guarantee smooth sailing for women in sports. With her brash attitude and androgynous style, Babe Didrikson, in particular, would upset those critics who required a certain degree of femininity in their female athletes. They wanted reassurance, such as that expressed by Lina Radke's doctor, that even though these women excelled at sports, they were not averse to cooking and sewing and cleaning like everyday housewives. Otherwise the expansion of women's sports threatened to blur the roles in a society where men prized being the strong, decision-making breadwinners and expected women to be their helpmates. The more unapologetic female athletes

were about their strength and competitive fire, the more they seemed to upset the balance of traditional male-female relations.

At the 1931 AAU track-and-field championships in Jersey City, New Jersey, Babe Didrikson sets a world record in the 80-meter hurdles (12 seconds flat). She also would set a world record in the baseball throw (296 feet—four feet shorter than a football field!).

Life in the United States and around the world changed drastically in late October 1929, when the stock market crashed and a decade-long economic depression began. But while these sobering times would lead to new challenges, they would not quash women's enthusiasm for or participation in sports. The trailblazing achievements of female athletes in the Roaring Twenties created a legacy that would inspire others for years to come even as the opposition continued and sometimes grew. There is a direct link from the athletes of the 1920s to every girl and woman who stands her ground today.

ALSO IN 1928–29

As the backlash to limit the participation of American women in sports started to take its toll in 1928 and 1929, Lou Henry Hoover and her husband headed to the White House. These years were a time of reckoning for the nation. A decade of reckless borrowing by investors had left the stock market on shaky ground, while the public's defiance of Prohibition had allowed powerful criminal organizations to flourish. Fortunately, there were some positive developments and even some lighthearted distractions to sustain the country in the rocky years ahead. Here are some noteworthy moments from 1928 and 1929.

1928

✷ MARGARET MEAD

AUGUST 23, 1928: Anthropologist Margaret Mead publishes *Coming of Age in Samoa*, a study based on her research with teenagers, especially teenage girls, on the island of Ta'ū in Samoa. Mead reports that the passage from childhood to adulthood is less difficult for Samoan girls than it is for American girls because Samoans are more open in their approach to sex and the body in general. She concludes that how an adult woman behaves depends on nurture (how she was raised) rather than on nature (preexisting natural laws). Although some would criticize her research, women in the United States who have been embracing new freedoms in careers, sports, and other aspects of life welcome Mead's findings because they seem to show that limits on women's roles are not predetermined.

Margaret Mead, 1935

Alexander Fleming working with penicillin mold in his lab

✷ DISCOVERING PENICILLIN

SEPTEMBER 28, 1928: Another breakthrough in the field of health takes place when Alexander Fleming, a Scottish scientist, discovers that spores of the *Penicillium chrysogenum* mold prevent the growth of bacteria. Fleming calls the antibacterial substance that the mold secretes "penicillin." Scientists would figure out how to mass produce penicillin in the 1940s, and it would become vital in limiting the number of deaths and amputations from infected wounds during World War II. After the war, it would become an important cure for bacterial infections in the population at large. For their work on penicillin, Fleming and two other scientists would win the 1945 Nobel Prize in medicine.

✷ HOOVER WINS

Herbert and Lou Henry Hoover, 1929

NOVEMBER 6, 1928: In a landslide victory, Republican Herbert Hoover defeats Alfred E. Smith to become the 31st president of the United States. Hoover, who is President Coolidge's secretary of commerce, wins support because of the booming economy. He also benefits from voter discrimination against Smith, who is Catholic. As first lady, Lou Henry Hoover's work with the Women's Division of the National Amateur Athletic Federation would take a back seat to her other duties. However, she would continue her affiliation with the Girl Scouts, championing their programs in frequent radio addresses. Not surprising, she would be a more activist first lady than her predecessors, supporting volunteerism, various social causes, and the arts.

✷ MASSACRE IN CHICAGO

FEBRUARY 14, 1929: The violence of the Prohibition era peaks with the St. Valentine's Day Massacre. Seven members and associates of a Chicago gang run by George "Bugs" Moran are gunned down by four assailants who allegedly work for rival gang boss Al Capone. Gangland violence has run rampant during Prohibition as criminal organizations have fought for control of the illegal liquor trade. But no city is as dangerous as Chicago, which has suffered upward of 400 gang murders a year. Capone is said to control all 10,000 speakeasies in the city and rule the bootlegging business from Canada to Florida. His reign would end in 1931, when he would go to prison for tax evasion.

Mug shot of Al Capone, early 1930s

1929

✷ POPULARIZING THE YO-YO

JUNE 9, 1928: Pedro Flores, a 29-year-old Filipino immigrant, founds the Yo-Yo Manufacturing Company in Santa Barbara, California. Although toys consisting of a disk on a string have existed for centuries, Flores bases his on a version popular in the Philippines. His "yo-yo"—a Tagalog term translated as "come-come"—has the string looped, instead of tied, around the axle. This allows the disk to stop moving before it returns to the operator, making tricks possible. Flores carves his first dozen wooden yo-yos by hand and generates interest by demonstrating tricks and holding yo-yo spinning contests at movie theaters. By March 1929, he has automated his factory and sold more than 100,000 yo-yos. Flores would sell his company to Donald F. Duncan, Sr., by 1932, but he would continue to promote the yo-yo all his life.

A young man judges female entrants in a yo-yo contest in 1932.

STAGE | BROADWAY | SCREEN

VARIETY

PRICE 25¢

VOL. XCVII. No. 3 | NEW YORK, WEDNESDAY, OCTOBER 30, 1929 | 88 PAGES

WALL ST. LAYS AN EGG

Going Dumb Is Deadly to Hostess In Her Serious Dance Hall Profesh

DROP IN STOCKS ROPES SHOWMEN

Kidding Kissers in Talkers Burns Up Fans of Screen's Best Lovers

Headline in *Variety* the day after the stock market crashed

✷ BLACK TUESDAY

OCTOBER 29, 1929: After showing signs of trouble for days, stock prices on the New York Stock Exchange collapse, ushering in a decade of economic hardship that would be known as the Great Depression. Stock prices had soared in the 1920s, driving many investors to buy shares "on margin," putting up as little as 10 percent and borrowing the rest from a bank or broker. When share prices fall, lenders demand their money and investors sell their stock at a loss, driving prices down even more. Sixteen million shares are sold on "Black Tuesday," and by mid-November, stocks would lose more than 40 percent of their total value. The Dow Jones Industrial Average of key stocks had peaked on September 3, 1929. It would not reach the same level again for 25 years.

EPILOGUE

— APPROACHING EQUALITY —

For much of the 20th century, girls in public schools had few opportunities to play sports. They had gym class, of course, and they could use their athletic talents as cheerleaders, rooting for boys. But unless they went to camp or joined a team through a community group or had fathers or brothers who took them under their wings, American girls were out of luck. Decades after Lou Henry Hoover first wielded her gavel as president of the Women's Division, her policy of steering girls away from competitive sports remained stubbornly in place. In the 1950s and '60s, most people didn't know *why* girls had so few athletic opportunities. They just accepted that sports were the province of boys.

Girls and women who pursued sports ran the risk of being seen as odd or unnatural. People questioned their sexuality. Reporters focused on their looks instead of their performances. A few sports organizations actually found success by emphasizing their players' femininity. In 1943, the All-American Girls Professional Baseball League sent its players to charm school to fine-tune their poise, and dressed them in impractical but revealing skirted uniforms. The result was a slew of articles with titles such as "Beauty at the Bat" and "World's Prettiest Ballplayers." But the league thrived for 12 years, giving 650 women the opportunity to play baseball at the highest level and serve as role models for generations to come.

Catcher Mary Baker of the All-American Girls Professional Baseball League often was referred to as "Pretty Bonnie Baker" in the press.

Meanwhile, black institutions consistently defied the prevailing views against women's competition. Black newspapers continued to applaud female

"Our culture's reverence for men's professional sports and its silence about women's athletic accomplishments shaped, defined, and limited how we felt about ourselves as women and men."

—Mariah Burton Nelson, *The Stronger Women Get, the More Men Love Football*, 1994

athletes and sponsor their teams. Tuskegee Institute added more events for women to its annual relays, with history-making results. In 1937, the Tuskegee women's track team won the national Amateur Athletic Union outdoor championship. It was the first time a historically black college won *any* national championship, but it wouldn't be the last. The women won 10 of the next 11 championships. Then, in 1960, a student from another historically black college, Tennessee State, almost single-handedly changed people's attitudes about the much maligned sport of women's track and field. That year's Olympics in Rome, Italy, were the first Summer Games ever televised worldwide. When viewers saw sprinter Wilma Rudolph's fluid, graceful style on her way to winning three gold medals, they started rethinking age-old objections to the sport.

Perhaps the greatest boon for female athletes came in 1972, when the U.S. Congress passed

Wilma Rudolph overcame childhood polio to win gold medals in the 100- and 200-meter sprints as well as the 4 × 100-meter relay (seen here) at the 1960 Summer Olympics.

Billie Jean King reaches for a shot in her match against Bobby Riggs on September 20, 1973.

the Education Amendments to the 1964 Civil Rights Act. Title IX of these amendments forbids institutions that receive federal funding from discriminating on the basis of sex. That meant schools had to provide girls with the same opportunities as boys, including in sports, or lose their federal support. Although there was a backlash from groups worried that more money spent on girls' sports would mean less money for the boys, Title IX dramatically changed the landscape of school athletics. In 1971–72, a total of 294,015 high school girls played interscholastic sports. By 2017–18, that number had risen to 3,415,306.

Soon after Title IX became law, another iconic event changed the perception of women athletes on a global scale. The Billie Jean King–Bobby Riggs tennis match, dubbed the "Battle of the Sexes," appealed to the fantasies of men who believed they could beat any female athlete, no matter how good she was. On September 20, 1973, more than 30,000 people crowded into Houston's Astrodome to witness the contest. Another 90 million watched on TV. When 29-year-old King beat 55-year-old Riggs in straight sets, 6–4, 6–3, 6–3, people everywhere started paying attention to women's sports. "There can be no doubt that Mrs. King's triumph," wrote Neil Amdur of the *New York Times,* "has strengthened her as the Joan of Arc of athletics, the one who raised her racquet for battle when few women challenged the broad inequalities inherent in the sports structure."

Progress was slow but steady after King's victory. By the 1990s, the first "Title IX generation"—women who benefited from the sports programs brought about by the law—were leading a new golden age of women's sports. The U.S. women's soccer team won the World Cup in 1991 and 1999 as well as a gold medal at the 1996 Olympic Games. U.S. women won gold in softball and basketball that year, too, and soon both sports had professional leagues. Women also fought for access to facilities where they had been denied entrance. One of the most well publicized struggles took place at Georgia's Augusta National Golf Club, home to the annual men's Masters Tournament. Women's groups launched a 10-year campaign to reverse the club's men-only policy. After losing sponsors for its tournaments because of this blatant discrimination, Augusta finally offered memberships to two women in 2012. In April 2019, the golf club strengthened its support of female

Pitcher Lisa Fernandez led the U.S. Olympic softball team to gold medals in 1996, 2000, and 2004, tallying a total of seven wins and one loss, as well as a .302 batting average.

golfers when it helped to create and host the Augusta National Women's Amateur Championship tournament.

Though there have been many victories, women have not yet achieved equity with men in sports. They have far fewer professional opportunities, and the pay scale for those that do exist is often dramatically lower. In 2017, *Forbes* magazine reported that the U.S. women's national soccer team was paid nearly four times less than the U.S. men's team despite bringing in more money and winning the 2015 World Cup. Two years later, 28 members of the women's team sued the sport's national governing body, U.S. Soccer, charging widespread bias that affected their pay, coaching, match schedules, travel and training budgets, and medical treatment. The team's fight for equity became a popular cause after the U.S. repeated as World Cup champions in 2019. Media coverage is another struggle for female athletes. A 2017 study by the University of Minnesota's Tucker Center found that although 40 percent of all sports participants were female, women only received 2 to 4 percent of all coverage.

Despite these continuing challenges, women's increased sports participation has had a powerful effect. It turns out that competing in sports is a character-building exercise that teaches athletes a lot more than how to

Megan Rapinoe led the powerful U.S. national team to its second consecutive World Cup championship in 2019, scoring a total of six goals and winning the Golden Boot, given to the tournament's top scorer, and the Golden Ball, for its best player.

Cynthia Cooper (14) earns MVP honors as she leads the Houston Comets to the first championship of the Women's National Basketball Association (WNBA) in 1997.

throw a ball or score a goal. It helps them learn how to work as part of a team, strategize, and come back after a defeat—essential skills in the workplace as well as on the playing field. A 2013 global study of business executives found that 90 percent of female senior managers played sports when they were younger. Although Lou Henry Hoover might not have foreseen women running PepsiCo or IBM or Sunoco, that is the reality now. Those leaders, and other girls and women today, owe a debt to the determined athletes of the 1920s who used sports to win more than championships. They shattered the stereotype of females as the weaker sex and proved that a woman can be as fit and fierce and in charge as any man.

DEFINING MOMENTS

— IN WOMEN'S SPORTS —

American women experienced lots of highs and lows in their journey toward sports glory. Here are 15 important turning points.

Artist Charles Dana Gibson, creator of the iconic Gibson Girl in the late 19th century, drew this female cyclist (left) for the June 1895 issue of *Scribner's* magazine.

1890s
Women Embrace the Bicycle › Before the bicycle craze captivated the nation in the 1890s, most women led sedentary lives, rendered inactive by social conventions and restrictive clothing. But women took to the two-wheeler in huge numbers, reveling in the opportunity to exercise, socialize, and break the bonds that held them back. This taste of freedom energized them for the century to come.

1909 **Auto Racing Bans Women ›** Just weeks after auto racer Joan Newton Cuneo set a new women's record for the mile (1 minute 1/5 second), the governing body of U.S. racing voted to ban women from competition, citing a concern for their safety. Women eventually found their way back to racing, but none drove in America's biggest contests, the Indianapolis 500 and the Daytona 500, until 1977. That year Janet Guthrie entered both, paving the way for Danica Patrick and other women with a passion for driving fast.

1926 **Ederle Conquers the Channel ›** In a year of huge sports stories, Gertrude Ederle made the biggest splash. No woman had ever successfully swum across the English Channel. Not only did Ederle succeed, but she also beat the existing men's record by almost two hours. When she returned home to New York, an estimated two million people greeted Ederle with the first ticker-tape parade ever to honor an individual female athlete. (Previous parades had honored men and women on U.S. Olympic teams.)

1928 **Runners Hit a Wall ›** In 1928, the IOC dealt a blow to women's track and field that would be felt for decades. Women's events were finally added to the Olympic program that year, only to be threatened with elimination after the press exaggerated the runners' level of fatigue at the end of a very competitive 800-meter race. After much debate, the women's 800 was eliminated from future Olympics, encouraging the myth that female runners could only handle short sprints. The race would not return until 1960.

1932 **Didrikson Dominates ›** Mildred "Babe" Didrikson was a new kind of female athlete: bold, brash, and undeterred by doubters or critics. Didrikson exploded into the public's consciousness at the 1932 Olympics, winning three medals—two gold and one silver—in track and field. She also excelled at basketball, baseball, and pretty much every other sport, finally turning to golf. She dominated pro tournaments until her death from cancer in 1956, at age 45.

Babe Didrikson

1950 **Gibson Triumphs ›** Althea Gibson became the first black athlete to break the color barrier in tennis when she competed at the U.S. National Tennis Championships at Forest Hills, New York, the precursor to the U.S. Open. She also became the first black player at Wimbledon in 1951, and the first to win singles at the French Championships, in 1956, and at Wimbledon and the U.S. Nationals, both in 1957. Not one to rest on her laurels, Gibson won both again in 1958.

Althea Gibson

1960 **Rudolph Blazes Ahead ›** With her blistering speed and graceful strides, sprinter Wilma Rudolph became the first woman ever to win three gold medals at a single Olympics. Her performance, at the first Summer Games televised worldwide, demonstrated the beauty of women's track to TV viewers, and caused many to reconsider their biases against the sport. Soon, physical educators started to encourage—and train—women to compete at the highest levels.

1967 **Switzer Runs the Boston Marathon ›** A year after Roberta "Bobbi" Gibb snuck in at the starting line to run the Boston Marathon, Kathrine Switzer became the first woman to officially register and run the race. Since the AAU prohibited women from competing in marathons, she signed up as "K. V. Switzer" and had her boyfriend pick up her number. Switzer finished the course, but she and others had to campaign for five more years before the AAU changed its rules.

1972 Title IX Levels the Playing Field › Before Title IX, female athletes had to contend with used equipment, part-time coaches, and other reminders that they were second-class citizens in the world of school sports. But the new law banned discrimination on the basis of sex in federally funded institutions, resulting in more teams, resources, and scholarships for women, and ultimately transforming the sports landscape in the United States.

1973 King Wallops Riggs › On paper, a tennis match pitting the 29-year-old reigning Wimbledon champion against a 55-year-old who was way past his prime didn't figure to be much of a contest. And it wasn't. But publicists and pundits called the match the Battle of the Sexes and somehow turned it into a referendum on women's rights. When Billie Jean King beat Bobby Riggs on September 20, 1973, women rejoiced and men started to rethink their prejudices toward women athletes and women in general.

1978 Lopez Thrills › No female golfer ever had as good a debut as Nancy Lopez. In 1978, her first full year as a pro, Lopez won nine tournaments including the LPGA Championship, her first major. She was named LPGA Rookie of the Year as well as Player of the Year, and won the Vare Trophy, named after Glenna Collett-Vare and given to the woman with the lowest scoring average for the season. Born in California of Mexican descent, Lopez kept playing—and winning—for two decades, fueling increased interest in women's golf along the way.

1982 NCAA Governs Women's Sports › Until the early 1980s, women's college sports were regulated by the Association for Intercollegiate Athletics for Women (AIAW), a group of female leaders. But then the men who ran the National Collegiate Athletic Association (NCAA) saw the financial potential of women's sports. The NCAA started offering its own women's tournaments, putting the AIAW out of business. This brought more visibility for female athletes, but it cost women control of their own sports programs. And as big-time women's teams offered higher salaries for coaches, more men took the jobs, denying female athletes role models of their own gender. The proportion of women's college teams with female coaches plummeted from more than 90 percent in 1974 to about 40 percent in 2017.

Nancy Lopez

1990s **Team Sports Come of Age ›** For much of the 20th century, most celebrated female athletes played individual sports, but in the 1990s, team sports came into their own. First the U.S. women's soccer team won the 1991 World Cup. Then American women took the gold in softball, basketball, and soccer at the 1996 Summer Olympics. And finally, the U.S. women's soccer team won the 1999 World Cup before a massive crowd of 90,185.

1998 **Book Calls Out Homophobia ›** Pat Griffin, a professor at the University of Massachusetts-Amherst, published *Strong Women, Deep Closets: Lesbians and Homophobia in Sport,* beginning a public dialogue on a topic that had long been discussed only in whispers. As far back as the 1920s, detractors used code words to express concerns about the sexuality of female athletes, questioning the "femininity" of any who exhibited uncommon strength or aggression. Over the years this implied disapproval led many athletes to hide their personal lives and others to play up their heterosexuality. Griffin's book looks at the history and social implications of homophobia with the goal of "opening minds, opening closet doors."

2017 **Gymnasts Stand Strong ›** Over 150 female gymnasts, including some Olympic gold medalists, showed a different kind of strength when they gave impact statements at the sentencing hearing of Dr. Larry Nassar, the sports doctor convicted of sexually assaulting them. Nassar was sentenced to 175 years in prison, and the U.S. Olympic Committee stepped in to reorganize the sport and make sure no gymnast would ever suffer any kind of abuse again.

Members of the U.S. national soccer team celebrate their 1999 World Cup win.

Rachael Denhollander, the first woman to publicly accuse Dr. Larry Nassar of sexual assault, testifies at his sentencing hearing in 2018.

AUTHOR'S NOTE

In some ways, *Breaking Through* is the culmination of my four-plus decades of researching and writing about women's sports history. I started way back in college, when I wrote a paper about three early tennis players: May Sutton Bundy, Molla Bjurstedt Mallory, and multisport athlete Eleonora Randolph Sears. I was amazed to learn there had been female tennis champions in the early 1900s. My history books never even hinted at that. It turned out to be one of many stories about women in general and female athletes in particular that had failed to register with the predominantly male authors who wrote the books we read when I was in school.

I set out to change that, in part because I felt there were so many stories that needed to be told, but also because I was looking for sports heroes beyond the major league baseball players I admired. Along the way, I had the thrill of meeting some of the women I wrote about, including two from the 1920s. I got Aileen Riggin's autograph in the late 1990s, when I met her at a fundraising event. She was in her early 90s, lovely and vibrant and a masters swimming champion in the 90–94 age group. I interviewed Margaret Gisolo, the baseball player from Indiana, in 2002, when she was 87 years old. She had recently retired as a college dance instructor and a seniors tennis champion.

It's also been meaningful to "discover" athletes who have been all but forgotten—"hidden figures" from the Roaring Twenties. Historians recently have started to write about Ora Washington and Izzy Channels, but Inez Patterson's story is still something of a mystery. I was determined to learn what I could about her and got some help from a Temple University student's prize-winning research paper on black women and basketball in the 1920s and 1930s (thank you, Charise Young!). I was unable to find Patterson's obituary, but I did discover an article from October 1944 reporting the recent hiring of a successor to "the late Inez Patterson" at the YWCA in Harlem, New York. Learning the year of her early death, however, brought up even more yet-to-be-answered questions about Patterson's life.

If information about these hidden figures is difficult to uncover, then usable photographs of them are nearly impossible to find. That's why we commissioned illustrations of Channels and Patterson. The illustrator based the portraits on grainy newspaper clippings from vintage black newspapers.

Writing nonfiction requires all sorts of detective work, and there's still more to do to get a complete picture of women's sports history in the 1920s. Black women were often left out of the mainstream media and the black newspapers that covered them have not been consistently archived like mainstream papers. But the historical record is virtually devoid of any mention of women from other backgrounds—for example, Asian Americans, Latinas, and Native Americans. I hope that people are inspired by the accounts of little-known athletes in this book and, as a result, organizations, institutions, and family members with evidence of sports participation among their female ancestors will come forward and share their stories. I look forward to the day when they are added to the narrative.

RESOURCES

BOOKS

■ **Cahn, Susan K.** *Coming on Strong: Gender and Sexuality in Twentieth-Century Women's Sport*. New York: The Free Press, 1994.

Cahn's groundbreaking analysis of the part gender and sexuality have played in the development of women's sports and the assessment of female athletes inspired many subsequent books, including this one.

■ **Gems, Gerald R., editor.** *Before Jackie Robinson: The Transcendent Role of Black Sporting Pioneers*. Lincoln, Nebraska: University of Nebraska Press, 2017.

This important collection of essays helps shed light on the lives and contributions of black athletes, including Izzy Channels, whose stories are absent from most traditional sports histories.

■ **Montillo, Roseanne.** *Fire on the Track: Betty Robinson and the Triumph of the Early Olympic Women*. New York: Crown, 2017.

Though it focuses on gold medal sprinter Betty Robinson, this volume gives an excellent overview of the 1928, 1932, and 1936 Summer Olympics and the bias against women in track and field.

■ **Mortimer, Gavin.** *The Great Swim*. New York: Walker and Company, 2008.

This well-researched book covers the frenzy as Gertrude Ederle and others attempt to swim the English Channel in 1926.

■ **Wiggins, David K., and Ryan A. Swanson, editors.** *Separate Games: African American Sport Behind the Walls of Segregation*. Fayetteville, Arkansas: University of Arkansas Press, 2016.

Articles in this cutting-edge history look at the *Philadelphia Tribune* women's basketball team, the Tennessee State Tigerbelles (Wilma Rudolph's track team), and the American Tennis Association, among many other topics.

WEBSITES

Black Tennis Hall of Fame
blacktennishistory.com/black-tennis-hall-of-fame

This is a rich source of material on tennis history, including photographs and biographies of the men and women who have been inducted into the hall, and articles about the American Tennis Association and black players.

"Only a Game" on National Public Radio
wbur.org/onlyagame/2018/08/31/basketball-hof-ora-washington

"The Nearly Forgotten History of Basketball HOF Inductee Ora Washington," by Karen Given, is just one of the terrific segments on sports history featured on this weekly radio program.

Women's Sports Foundation
womenssportsfoundation.org

The website of this advocacy organization contains lots of information about the history and impact of Title IX as well as material on current female athletes.

YouTube
YouTube.com

You can go back in time on YouTube and watch some of the athletic performances by the women mentioned in this book, including:

- Aileen Riggin's springboard dive at the 1920 Olympics: *youtube.com/watch?v=nlNq2xeisYo*
- Helen Wills playing Suzanne Lenglen in 1926: *youtube.com/watch?v=P6xiG4_rAmQ*
- Wilma Rudolph's three gold medal runs in 1960: *youtube.com/watch?v=FPVdpJZJi-o*

QUOTE SOURCES AND NOTES

CHAPTER 1

p. 12: "There were no ... who had won." Aileen Riggin, interview by Dr. Margaret Costa, LA84 Foundation, November 11, 1994, accessed July 3, 2018, at digital.la84.org/digital/collection/p17103coll11/id/241/rec/3; "women's suffrage ... law of the land." Tennessee became the 36th state to ratify the 19th Amendment on August 18, 1920, satisfying the necessary 3/4 of the 48 states in the Union.

p. 13: "She got ... summer." Riggin interview, op. cit.; "27 million ... state of the Union." *With Courage and Cloth: Winning the Fight for a Woman's Right To Vote* by Ann Bausum, National Geographic, 2004, pp. 66, 83; "was opposed ... long skirts." "No Women Athletes for American Team," *New York Times*, March 31, 1914, p. 9; "the dictator ... this country." "Wray's Column," by John E. Wray, *St. Louis Post-Dispatch*, June 16, 1914, p. 10.

p. 13 Note: Although the 19th Amendment granted women across the U.S. the right to vote, not all women automatically had access to the ballot box. For example, Native Americans were not granted U.S. citizenship until 1924 and some states disenfranchised them well into the 1950s. Meanwhile, a number of Southern states undermined the voting rights of black citizens into the 1960s. Voting rights are still being threatened in some states.

p. 14: "America's ... Work." "J.E. Sullivan Dies After an Operation," *New York Times*, September 17, 1914, p. 9; "purposeful dehydration" "The 1904 Olympic Marathon May Have Been the Strangest Ever," by Karen Abbott, Smithsonian.com, August 7, 2012, accessed July 22, 2018, smithsonianmag.com/history/the-1904-olympic-marathon-may-have-been-the-strangest-ever-14910747/#CylMh2ilkqHDEmGg.99; "formed ... male sex." "Women Barred by the A.A.U.," *Boston Globe*, January 18, 1914, p. 15; "Our women ... no rivals." "Comment on Current Events in Sports: Women in Water Sports," *New York Times*, July 17, 1916, p. 8.

p. 15: "At the beginning ... to the trunk." "Testimony from Colleges: Vassar," by Alida C. Avery, in *Sex and Education: A Reply to Dr. E.H. Clarke's "Sex in Education,"* Julia Ward Howe, editor, Roberts Brothers, 1874, pp. 192–193.

p. 16: "When Clara ... miss her!" and "a moral ... of muscle!" "Woman as an Athlete," by Dr. Arabella Kenealy, *The Living Age*, February 29, 1899, pp. 366, 369.

p. 17: "It's the ... deny it." "Hot Shot for 'Jim' Sullivan," *New York Times*, July 19, 1913, p. 5; "The Most Athletic ... darning socks." "The Most Athletic Mother on Earth," *Wichita Daily Times* (Wichita Falls, Texas), November 20, 1921, p. 15.

p. 20: "Some people ... of competition." "The Right Kind of Athletics for Girls," by Florence A. Summers, *American Physical Education Review*, June 1916, p. 373. (The journal misspelled the author's last name. It is actually Somers.)

p. 21: "every state required ... intercollegiate team." Statistics cited in "Toward a New Sporting Ideal: The Women's Division of the National Amateur Athletic Federation," by Nancy Theriot, *Frontiers: A Journal of Women Studies*, Spring 1978, p. 2; "The big joke ... circles." "College Chatter," *Evening News* (Harrisburg, Pennsylvania), December 7, 1921, p. 22.

p. 22: Introduction: "85 percent ... in 1920," "Table A-12. Race for the United States, Regions, Divisions, and States: 1920," in "Historical Census Statistics on Population Totals by Race, 1790 to 1990, and by Hispanic Origin, 1970 to 1990, for the United States, Regions, Divisions, and States," by Campbell Gibson and Kay Jung, Population Division Working Paper No. 56, U.S. Bureau of the Census, 2002, accessed April 2, 2019, mapmaker.rutgers.edu/REFERENCE/Hist_Pop_stats.pdf.

p. 23: Radio Station: "556 by 1923" "The History of the Radio Industry in the United States to 1940," by Carole E. Scott, EH.net, Economic History Association, accessed October 3, 2018, eh.net/encyclopedia/the-history-of-the-radio-industry-in-the-united-states-to-1940/.

CHAPTER 2

p. 26: "the game ... encouraged" and "They certainly ... goodness." Scott, pp. 49, 58; "The women ... to be desired." "English Girls Lose at Soccer in U.S.," *New York Times*, September 25, 1922.

p. 27: "We give no ... ask none." "Girl Soccerists Tackle D.C. Male Eleven Today," *Evening Star*, Washington, D.C., October 8, 1922, p. 72.

p. 28: "I have my school ... in the world!" "Why I'd Rather Teach School Than Star in the Movies," *Austin* (Texas) *American*, March 23, 1923, p. 32; "Ever since ... with dolls." "She Won for U.S.," by Bob Dorman, *Hutchinson* (Kansas) *Gazette*, September 7, 1922, p. 2.

p. 29: "The time ... athletics." AAU President William C. Prout, quoted in "The Controlled Development of Collegiate Sport for Women, 1923–1936," by Ellen Gerber, *Journal of Sport History*, 1975, p. 6; "the making and breaking ... organizations." "Policy and Platform" brochure quoted in "An Uncommon Woman: The Quiet Leadership Style of Lou Henry Hoover," by Dale C. Mayer, *Presidential Studies Quarterly*, Fall 1990, p. 690.

p. 30: "A sport ... in a sport." "Women's Struggle for Governance in U.S. Amateur Athletics," by Joan S. Hult, *International Review for the Sociology of Sport*, September 1989, p. 251; "the development ... [female] sex." J. Anna Norris, 1924, quoted in Gerber, p. 15.

p. 31: "Amid cheers ... competition." "A Southern California Sports Day," by Marian E. Pettit, *The Sportswoman*, May 1, 1926, pp. 12–13.

p. 32 Note: The National Association of College Women wasn't the only organization for black women with the acronym NACW. The National Association of Colored Women was founded in 1896 by Harriet Tubman, Mary Church Terrell, and others to provide a platform for black women to serve as leaders in their communities. That NACW campaigned for suffrage and against lynching and Jim Crow laws, which enforced racial segregation.

p. 33: "smoking drives ... the world." "National Women's Champion Could Hold Own With Suzanne Lenglen, Says Edgar Brown," by Edgar G. Brown, *Pittsburgh Courier*, June 2, 1923, p. 7; "scoring and ... her colleagues." The *Chicago Defender* quoted in "Isadore Channels: The Recovered Life of a Great African American Sports Star," by Robert Pruter, in *Before Jackie Robinson: The Transcendent Role of Black Sporting Pioneers,"* edited by Gerald R. Gems, University of Nebraska Press, 2017.

p. 34: "enlightened whites ... championship." Tally Holmes quoted in "Game, Set, and Separatism: The American Tennis Association, A Tennis Vanguard," by Sundiata Djata, in *Separate Games: African American Sport Behind the Walls of Segregation*, edited by David K. Wiggins and Ryan A. Swanson, University of Arkansas Press, 2016, p. 166; "The muscular man ... beautiful form." "Women Athletes Eyesore on Beauty Landscape, Warns Prominent Artist," *The Courier* (Waterloo, Iowa), January 25, 1923, p. 2.

p. 35: "severe violence ... mature women." "Will Women Athletes Mean More Empty Cradles?" by Arthur C. Jacobson, *San Francisco Chronicle*, May 13, 1923, p. 7.

p. 37: Emily Post: "a fellowship ... gentle-folk." "How To Behave When You Get in the '400'," *Philadelphia Inquirer*, July 23, 1922, Feature Section, p. 3.

CHAPTER 3

p. 39: "We play ... hockey." "Ladies Armed with Clubs," by Drew C. Pendergrass, *Fifteen Minutes Magazine*, December 1, 2016, accessed August 30, 2018, thecrimson.com/article/2016/12/1/constance-applebee-harvard/.

p. 41: "a woman's magazine ... achievements." "Editorials," *The Sportswoman*, September 1, 1924; "Through its columns ... activities." "Advertisement," ibid.

p. 42: "Women have but ... prohibited." Coubertin quoted in *Female Olympians: A Mediated Socio-Cultural and Political-Economic Timeline*, by Linda K. Fuller, Palgrave Macmillan, 2016, p. 27; "She never missed ... the course." February 22, 1925, quoted in "They Are Women, Hear Them Roar: Female Sportswriters of the Roaring Twenties," a thesis in mass communications by David Kaszuba, Pennsylvania State University, 2003, p. 67, accessed March 3, 2019, etda.libraries.psu.edu/catalog/6174.

p. 43: "who loves ... eat candy." Kaszuba, p. 69.

p. 45: "This American schoolgirl ... achievement." "A Great Champion," *Chicago Tribune*, August 26, 1924, p. 6.

p. 46: "Miss Wills ... Pickford." "10,000 See Helen Wills Win Straight Set Victory Over Molla Mallory for U.S. Title," by Vincent Richards, *El Paso* (Texas) *Times*, August 17, 1924, p. 9; "ten individuals ... in all sport." "The Sportlight," by Grantland Rice, *Courier-Post* (Camden, New Jersey), December 29, 1924, p. 12; "Miss Washington ... male players." "Reid Is Victor at Lawnside Tourney," *Courier-Post*, August 11, 1925, p. 13.

p. 47: "the best ... the world." *American Women's Track and Field: A History, 1895 Through 1980, Volume 1*, by Louise Mead Tricard, McFarland, 1996, p. 106; "She runs ... twinkle merrily." "World's Champion Girl Athlete Was Invalid Three Years Ago," by Lincoln Quarberg, *Daily Times* (Longmont, Colorado), August 1, 1925.

p. 48: "The so-called ... points of the game." "Girls' Floor League To Be Organized," *Pittsburgh Courier*, September 19, 1925, p. 13.

p. 49: "to reconcile ... wanted to see." *Coming on Strong: Gender and Sexuality in Twentieth-Century Women's Sports*, by Susan K. Cahn, The Free Press, 1994, p. 211; "Dora can sew ... cook." "Dora Lurie Best Fair Basketeer," by Gordon MacKay, *Philadelphia Inquirer*, February 1924, p. 20; "No bobbed hair ... 'Good fellow.'" "The Paragon," *Salt Lake* (City, Utah) *Telegram*, September 21, 1924, p. 23. "No matter ... to matter." and "If there is ... never seen it." Paul Gallico, *Farewell to Sport*, 1937, quoted in "Remembering Paul Gallico, The Sportswriter Who Hated Women But Was Okay With Nazis," by Dave McKenna, Deadspin.com, December 29, 2015, accessed March 4, 2019, deadspin.com/remembering-paul-gallico-the-sports writer-who-hated-wo-1749309043.

CHAPTER 4

p. 54: "Movie rights ... $100,000." "$100,000 for Movie Rights To Wills-Lenglen Meeting," *New York Times*, February 9, 1926, p. 20; "It seems ... speculators." "Money Fever Rules Riviera Tennis," by Don Skene, *Daily News* (New York, New York), February 10, 1926, p. 116; "Never has ... authority." "Riviera Background," by John Tunis, originally published in the *Boston Globe*, February 14, 1926, reprinted in *The Fireside Book of Tennis*, edited by Allison Danzig and Peter Schwed, Simon and Schuster, 1972, p. 141.

p. 55: "Suzanne's game ... did ordinarily." "Sports of the Times: Tennis Battle of Century," by Allison Danzig, *New York Times*, August 7, 1960, section 5, p. 2.

p. 56: "howling, yelling ... not what for" and "which ... to play" and "competition ... takes part." "Safeguarding Girls' Athletics," by Blanche M. Trilling, excerpts from an address given before the Annual Meeting of the National Association of Deans of Women, Dallas, Texas, February, 1927, published in *Women and Athletics*, Women's Division, NAAF, A.S. Barnes and Company, Inc., 1930, pp. 10, 11, 13; "The Channel ... of nature." George Trevor, the *Sun* (New York, New York), August 4, 1926, quoted in *The Great Swim*, by Gavin Mortimer, Walker and Company, 2008, p. 124.

p. 58: "The beauty ... teach people a lesson!" *Herald Tribune*, August 7, 1926, quoted in Mortimer, p. 163.

p. 59: "The early death ... shortening life." "Today," by Arthur Brisbane, *Star and Times* (St. Louis, Missouri), February 1, 1927, p. 2.

p. 60: "The *Pittsburgh Courier* ... set high marks." "Ellen Ray To Attempt 17-Mile Swim as 'Miss Courier,'" by Floyd J. Calvin, *Pittsburgh Courier*, February 5, 1927, p. 12.

p. 61: "Which was ... probably forever." and "Men, it seems, ... and stamina!" "Why Men Beat Women at Sports," by Arthur Grahame, *Popular Science Monthly*, November 1926, pp. 30, 154.

p. 62 Note: In the Japanese culture, a person's family name—what in America is consider the last name—usually appears first. Although the press referred to the star of the 1926 Women's World Games as Kinue Hitomi, she was known as Hitomi Kinue in Japan.

p. 64: Book of the Month: "more than 100 million books" "Book-of-the-Month Club, Inc.," Company-Histories.com, accessed January 3, 2019, company-histories.com/BookoftheMonth-Club-Inc-Company-History.html; Annie Oakley: "With the ... frontier is gone." "Annie Oakley Passes," Editorial, *Democrat and Chronicle* (Rochester, New York), November 4, 1926, p. 14.

p. 65: *Homespun Heroines*: "her house served ... Underground Railroad." *Black Pioneers in Communication Research*, by Ronald L. Jackson II and Sonja M. Brown Givens, Sage Publications, Inc., 2006, p. 66.

CHAPTER 5

p. 67: "The 800-metre ... for the distance." "Canada Takes Two Places in Girls' 800-Metre Event," by W. H. Ingram, *The Gazette* (Montreal, Canada), August 3, 1928, p. 13; " Radke ... Japanese runner." "Yankee Eight Beats Belgium in Boat Crew," by Associated Press, *Leader-Telegram* (Eau Claire, Wisconsin), August 3, 1928, p. 8.

p. 68: "The final ... off the track." "Americans Beaten in 4 Olympic Tests," by Wythe Williams, *New York Times*, August 3, 1928, p. 11.

p. 69: "sensibility and attention ... acts of charity." "Pope States Stand on Girl Athletes," *New York Times*, May 4, 1928, p. 7; "parents must keep ... modestly dressed." "Policy of Women's Dress," *Daily Notes* (Canonsburg, Pennsylvania), March 3, 1930, p. 4.

p. 70: "the world champion ... *hausfrau*." "Women's Events: Restriction of Distance," *Morning Herald* (Sydney, Australia), August 9, 1928, p. 11; "I would not ... last Olympics." Ethel Perrin quoted in "Circumspice!," *The Sportswoman*, February 1929, p. 15; "to do all ... on winning." *American Women's Track and Field: A History, 1895 Through 1980*, by Louise Mead Tricard, McFarland and Company, 1996, p. 158.

p. 71: "The Central Board ... plans for one." Tricard et al., pp. 159–160.

p. 73: "I always refused ... at that time." "Temple Student Tells How She Met Swim Color Bar," by Bernice Dutrieuille, *Afro-American* (Baltimore, Maryland), June 23, 1934, quoted in "African American Women's Basketball in the 1920s and 1930s: Active Participants in the 'New Negro' Movement," by Charise Young, Temple University, December 9, 2009, p. 19; "foremost girl ... city." *Philadelphia Tribune*, January 21, 1931, quoted in "The Philadelphia Tribune Newsgirls," by J. Thomas Jable, in *Separate Games*, op. cit. p. 41; "two of the greatest ... Depression." "A Resolution Honoring Philadelphia Tennis and Basketball Legend (Ora Washington)," accessed April 10, 2019, phlcouncil.com/gym-orawashington-resolution.

p. 74: "The rules ... for a girl." "Girl Star Created Biggest Headache on Eligibility Rule," by Dan Sowers, *Sporting News Junior Baseball Edition*, May 1948.

p. 75: "to promote ... aviation." "86 Women Pilots In Country Form New Association," *Atlanta Constitution*, December 16, 1929, p. 16. (The group was originally called the Eighty-Sixes, but was changed to the Ninety-Nines after more women joined.)

p. 79: Yo-Yos: "more than 100,000 yo-yos" *Distinguished Asian American Business Leaders*, by Naomi Hirahara, Greenwood Publishing Group, 2003, p. 57; Massacre: "all 10,000 ... to Florida." *This Fabulous Century: Volume III, 1920-1939*, by the Editors of Time-Life Books, Time Inc., 1969, p. 175; Black Tuesday: "more than 40 percent ... value." *American History: A Survey: Volume II: Since 1865* (Fourth Edition), by Richard N. Current, T. Harry Williams, and Frank Freidel, Alfred A. Knopf, 1975, p. 655.

EPILOGUE

p. 80: "Beauty at the Bat ... Ballplayers." "Beauty at the Bat" by James Gordon, *American Magazine*, June 1945, pp. 24–25, and "World's Prettiest Ballplayers" by Carl L. Biemiller, *Holiday*, June 1952, pp. 50+.

p. 82: "In 1971–72 ... 3,415,306." "2017–18 High School Athletics Participation Survey Results," National Federation of State High School Associations, accessed October 19, 2018, nfhs.org/ParticipationStatistics/ParticipationStatistics.

p. 83: "90 million watched on TV." "Battle of the Sexes: A Guide to the Legendary Tennis Match Between Billie Jean King and Bobby Riggs," by Ryan Bort, *Newsweek*, September 22, 2017, accessed October 19, 2018, newsweek.com/battle-sexes-guide-billie-jean-king-bobby-riggs-669300; "There can be ... sports structure." "'She Played Too Well,' Says Riggs of Mrs. King," by Neil Amdur, *New York Times*, September 22, 1973, pp. 21, 24.

p. 84: "In 2017, *Forbes* ... most recent World Cup." "Soccer's Ridiculous Gender Wage Gap [Infographic]," by Niall McCarthy, *Forbes*, November 28, 2017, accessed November 10, 2018, forbes.com/sites/niallmccarthy/2017/11/28/soccers-ridiculous-gender-wage-gap-infographic/#743375c57b08; "A 2017 study ... of all coverage." "Progress and Inequality: Women's Sports and the Gender Gap," by Mary Jo Kane, *Improving Lives: College of Education and Human Development Vision 2020 Blog*, accessed November 10, 2018, cehdvision2020.umn.edu/blog/progress-inequality-womens-sports-gender-gap.

p. 85: "A 2013 global study ... were younger." Survey by Ernst & Young's Women Athletes Business Network reported in "What Do Sports Teach Women for Business?" by Hadley Catalano, theGlasshammer.com, accessed October 19, 2018, theglasshammer.com/2014/04/22/what-do-sports-teach-women-for-business/.

DEFINING MOMENTS

p. 88: "The proportion of ... 40 percent in 2017." "Number of Women Coaching in College Has Plummeted in Title IX Era," by Jere Longman, *New York Times*, March 30, 2017.

ILLUSTRATION CREDITS

GI: Getty Images; LCPPD: Library of Congress Prints and Photographs Division; SS: Shutterstock

Cover, Bettmann/GI; Back cover, Addison N. Scurlock/Nannie Helen Burroughs Collection/LCPPD; Flap, Adam Glickman/Underwood Archives/GI; 1, Underwood Archives/GI; 2-3, Chicago Sun-Times/Chicago Daily News collection/Chicago History Museum/GI; 4-5, Hulton-Deutsch Collection/Corbis/GI; 7, David E. Klutho/Sports Illustrated/GI; 9, Sheila Wolinsky; 10, Underwood & Underwood, N.Y./Wittemann Collection/LCPPD; 12, Bettmann Archive/GI; 13, Universal History Archive/UIG/GI; 14, The Miriam and Ira D. Wallach Division of Art, Prints and Photographs/The New York Public Library; 15, Archives & Special Collections, Vassar College Library, Archives 08.17; 16, Norman Batho Collection; 17, Adam Glickman/Underwood Archives/GI; 18, Gocili/SS; 19, Katherine E.McClellan/Smith College; 20, Universal History Archive/UIG /GI; 21, Marquisphoto/SS; 22 (UP), ullstein bild/GI; 22 (LO), LCPPD; 23 (UP LE), Chicago History Museum/GI; 23 (LO LE), Bettmann Archive/GI; 23 (UP RT), Victoria Arocho/AP/REX/SS; 23 (LO RT), Bettmann Archive/GI; 24, ullstein bild/GI; 26, Historia/REX/SS; 27, Bibliothèque Nationale de France; 28, Paul Thompson/FPG/GI; 29, National Photo Company Collection/LCPPD; 30, Naci Yavuz/SS; 31, Michael Ochs Archives/GI; 32, Corbis/Bettmann Archive/GI; 33, Tristan Elwell; 34, Brocreative/SS; 35, Bettmann Archive/GI; 36 (UP), Solodov Aleksei/SS; 36 (LO), Fotosearch/GI; 37 (UP LE), LCPPD; 37 (UP RT), Mediapunch/SS; 37 (LO LE), Jaroslav Moravcik/SS; 37 (LO RT), Historia/REX/SS; 38, National Photo Company Collection/LCPPD; 41, Mavis/SS; 42, ullstein bild/GI; 43, Topical Press Agency/Hulton Archive/GI; 44-45, Popperfoto/GI; 45, Allsport Hulton/Archive/GI; 46, Hulton Archive/GI; 47, Bettmann Archive/GI; 48, John W. Mosley Photography Collection, Charles L. Blockson Afro-American Collection, Temple University Libraries, Philadelphia, PA; 49, Keystone-France\Gamma-Rapho via GI; 50 (UP), LCPPD; 50 (LO), National Photo Company Collection/LCPPD; 51 (UP LE), Everett Historical/SS; 51 (LO LE), Joseph Sohm/SS; 51 (UP RT), AP/REX/SS; 51 (LO RT), Bettmann Archive/GI; 52, Bettmann Archive/GI; 54, Bettmann Archive/GI; 55, kstudija/SS; 56, Courtesy of the University of Wisconsin–Madison Archives (ID ch05072202); 57, NY Daily News Archive/GI; 58, AP/REX/SS; 59, Bob Thomas/Popperfoto/GI; 60, Hulton-Deutsch Collection/Corbis/GI; 62, The Asahi Shimbun/GI; 63, Minnesota Historical Society/Corbis/GI; 64 (LE), Thomas Bethge/SS; 64 (RT), Historia/REX/SS; 65 (UP LE), William Henry Richards Collection within the Robert H. McNeill Family Collections/LCPPD; 65 (LO LE), AP/REX/SS; 65 (UP RT), AP/REX/SS/GI; 65 (LO RT), Bettmann Archive/GI; 66, Kyodo News/GI; 68, Colorsport/REX/SS; 69, Carl Simon/United Archives/UIG/GI; 70, Bokica/SS; 71, Bettmann Archive/GI; 72, George Rinhart/Corbis/GI; 73, Tristan Elwell; 74, Bettmann Archive/GI; 75, LCPPD; 76, Carl Simon/United Archives/UIG/GI; 77, Underwood Archives/REX/SS; 78 (UP), AP/REX/SS; 78 (LO), New York World-Telegram and the Sun Newspaper Photograph Collection/LCPPD; 79 (UP LE), National Photo Company Collection/LCPPD; 79 (UP RT), Universal History Archive/UIG/REX/SS; 79 (LO LE), Hulton-Deutsch Collection/Corbis/GI; 79 (LO RT), Bettmann Archive/GI; 80, courtesy of the author; 81, AP/REX/SS; 82, Neil Leifer /Sports Illustrated/GI; 83, Eric Draper/AP/REX/SS; 84, Paul Currie/BPI/SS; 85, Nathaniel S. Butler/NBAE/GI; 86, Charles Dana Gibson/LCPPD; 87 (UP), ANL/REX/SS; 87 (LO), AP/REX/SS; 88, Dunn/AP/REX/SS; 89 (UP), David Madison/GI; 89 (LO), Rena Laverty/EPA-EFE/REX/SS

INDEX

Illustrations are indicated by **boldface.**

For Marty Ittner, brilliant designer.
I couldn't do these without you.

Acknowledgments

This is my seventh book for National Geographic, and although some of the players behind the scenes have changed over the years, I continue to feel privileged to publish with a house that values women's history and pulls out all the stops to make books that matter. So thanks to the in-house staff for this book: editor Paige Towler, photo director Lori Epstein, art director Callie Broaddus, editorial director Becky Baines, and the rest of the team, as well as my brilliant independent colleagues, editor Suzanne Fonda and designer Marty Ittner. Each of you played a vital role in putting this book together.

I am grateful that Muffet McGraw, the exceptional head coach of Notre Dame's championship women's basketball team, accepted our invitation to write the foreword for this book. Thanks also to sports historian Susan Cahn for her pioneering work and for lending her expertise as our consultant, and to Michele Mitchell for her thoughtful review of the manuscript. And thanks to my mom and my brother for their love and encouragement, to Estelle Freedman for her continued inspiration, to Shannon Savage for understanding, and to Jackie Glasthal for helping me find my way.

Since 1888, the National Geographic Society has funded more than 12,000 research, exploration, and preservation projects around the world. The Society receives funds from National Geographic Partners, LLC, funded in part by your purchase. A portion of the proceeds from this book supports this vital work. To learn more, visit natgeo.com/info.

NATIONAL GEOGRAPHIC and Yellow Border Design are trademarks of the National Geographic Society, used under license.

For more information, visit nationalgeographic.com, call 1-877-873-6846, or write to the following address:

National Geographic Partners
1145 17th Street N.W.
Washington, DC 20036-4688 U.S.A.

Visit us online at nationalgeographic.com/books

For librarians and teachers: ngchildrensbooks.org

More for kids from National Geographic: natgeokids.com

National Geographic Kids magazine inspires children to explore their world with fun yet educational articles on animals, science, nature, and more. Using fresh storytelling and amazing photography, *Nat Geo Kids* shows kids ages 6 to 14 the fascinating truth about the world—and why they should care. kids.nationalgeographic.com/subscribe

For information about special discounts for bulk purchases, please contact National Geographic Books Special Sales: specialsales@natgeo.com

For rights or permissions inquiries, please contact National Geographic Books Subsidiary Rights: bookrights@natgeo.com

Designed by Marty Ittner

Hardcover ISBN: 978-1-4263-3676-8
Reinforced library binding ISBN: 978-1-4263-3677-5

Printed in China
19/PPS/1